Mary Schoeser is a recognized
advised organizations such as E
of London and the Metropolitan
a research fellow at Central Sain
Her publications cover the full ra
entries in *Materials and Techniqu* .... *An illustrated*
Dictionary (2002) to a survey of contemporary work in *International Textile*
Design (1995).

THAMES & HUDSON INC.
500 Fifth Avenue
New York, New York 10110

Printed in Singapore

Mary Schoeser

World Textiles

A Concise History

210 illustrations, 106 in color

 Thames & Hudson world of art

To Terry, who forgives my round-the-clock writing

1. (previous page) 18th-century embroidered velvet Koran folder

© 2003 Thames & Hudson Ltd, London

First published in paperback in the United States of America in 2003 by Thames & Hudson Inc., 500 Fifth Avenue, New York, New York 10110

thamesandhudsonusa.com

Library of Congress Catalog Card Number 2002110919
ISBN 0-500-20369-5

Printed and bound in Singapore by C. S. Graphics

Contents

Introduction

A comparison between prehistoric and present-day textiles demonstrates the lack of logic in a linear history, which takes us from simple to complex, or from plain to patterned. Many of the materials, techniques and forms used in ancient times remain in use today, both as essential aspects of production in many regions of the world and as ingredients in textile arts. Such continuity makes textiles unique among all artifacts. The fact that their making often involves the creation of the 'ingredients' – unlike working with wood or stone – makes them extremely complex and particularly revealing of human ingenuity. It can be argued that as indicators of cultural mechanisms, textiles offer insights into the greatest range of developments, embracing not only technology, agriculture and trade, but also ritual, tribute, language, art and personal identity.

The relationship of textiles to writing is especially significant, not only for the cuneiform-like qualities of many patterns, but also for the parallels between ink on papyrus and pigment on bark cloth. There is, in fact, little difference between the two. Such connections are implied in many textile terms. For example, the Indian full-colour painted and printed 'kalamkari' are so named from the Persian for pen, *kalam*; the wax for Indonesian batiks is delivered by a copper-bowled *tulis*, also meaning pen. The European term for hand-colouring of details on cloth is 'pencilling'. And the Islamic term *tiraz*, originally denoting embroideries, came to encompass all textiles within this culture that carried inscriptions. With or without inscriptions, textiles convey all kinds of 'texts': allegiances are expressed, promises are made (as in today's bank notes, whose value is purely conceptual), memories are preserved, new ideas are proposed. Many anthropological

2. Being both functional and decorative, textiles can be read in many ways. This wallpocket of 1710–30 displays figures representing Faith, Hope and Charity, and the Four Cardinal Virtues as identified by Plato. It has significance for studies of classicism, Christianity, Western concepts of women, and the role of needlework in a young woman's education. Made of plain silk taffeta, silk floss, silver and gilt thread and gold lace and braid, it also documents the fine materials then available in Engadine (Grisons canton, Switzerland), as well as the skills and taste of its maker.

and ethnographical studies of textiles aim at teaching us how to read these cloth languages anew. The 'plot' is provided by the socially meaningful elements; the 'syntax' is the construction, often only revealed by the application of archaeological and conservation analyses. Equally, the most creative textiles of today exploit a vocabulary of fibres, dyes and techniques. Textiles can be prose or poetry, instructive or the most demanding of texts. The ways in which they are used – and reused – add more layers of meaning, all significant indicators of sensitivities that can be traced back at least ten thousand years.

Taking a lead from textiles also engenders a more balanced understanding of the indigenous cultures that never developed the use of bronze and iron (as in Australia), developed iron use alone and comparatively late (as in Africa in about 800 BC), or developed the use of copper followed rapidly by iron (as in the Americas in about AD 100). That said, there *is* a relationship between metallurgical skills and textile-making. As the climate warmed at the end of the last Ice Age (*c.* 7000 BC), the loss of abundant vegetation in certain areas forced communities to redirect observational and manipulatory skills in order to settle and to control and preserve food supplies. These skills were already highly developed through centuries of experience with textile materials and techniques, and their contribution to agriculture and animal husbandry can be readily deduced, not merely in the use of cordage and bands for ploughs and reins, but, more significantly, in the way such concepts were expressed: 'haft', for example, means not only 'to bind' and 'handle', but also to habituate animals to a new pasture. In light of all this, could not the same skills have contributed to the development of metallurgy? Certainly metallurgy and textile techniques later become closely related through their joint applications in machine-building and as a result of the lead taken in organic chemistry by first dye, and then fibre, sciences.

The aim of this book is not to give a country-by-country account of textiles (although a guide to geographical and cultural groupings can be found in the Geographical Index), but to sketch in the themes discussed above to explore the worldwide connections and influences that have made textiles global commodities for centuries. This focus means that the important and generally interconnected topics of materials, methods, trade, technology and social structures are not constantly cross-referred. Instead, each of these subjects is twice highlighted in the following ten chapters to suggest their continued pertinence. In building a doorway to this subject, I make no apologies for this personal choice – based both on what I know and on what I know to be less thoroughly charted – and for making only passing reference to what will be readily accessible to readers elsewhere. Thus, fashion and other means of consumption of textiles, gender issues, aesthetic characteristics and individuals do not figure prominently here. In addition, since academic and popular publications on this subject were until recently dominated by European and North American publishers, source material must be understood to be Western in bias, even when the topic is non-Western. Finally, in a survey such as this the repetitive citation of exceptions to the rule was felt to be unwieldy, and it is easier to note at the outset that the statements that follow almost always have a caveat or two. This reflects the richness and diversity of textiles, a subject so vast that there remain numerous avenues to be explored, some of which are suggested in the following pages.

Chapter 1:   Prehistoric Materials and Techniques

The first needles are associated with the European Gravettian culture (26,000–20,000 BC) and its roughly contemporary counterpart, the Eastern Gravettian, which includes all mammoth-hunting peoples of eastern Europe and Russia. Needles allowed the joining of skins, and are one of the tools that distinguish the Gravettian from its preceding culture, the Aurignacian (the first Upper Paleolithic culture, which is known to have made pins from polished bone or antler). Together with Gravettian awls and punches, needles – some with relatively fine eyes – also made possible the joining together of numerous found objects such as pierced pebbles, shells, seeds and teeth. Many of these would have been strung on strands as jewellers do today. Others, as in the Grotte des Enfants cave burials in southern France, were placed with such precision across the skull that they must have been fixed to a supporting structure, whether a headband, cap or hairnet. This chapter explores how such supports might have been constructed by considering the basic necessity – thread or cordage – and the range of manipulative techniques common to all cultures. These techniques were known long before pottery and in many cultures continued into modern times as the principal means of creating useful, decorative and symbolic objects.

Undoubtedly the first textile art was the creation of threads, yarns and cords, distinguished from one another by their diameters, from fine to thick. Beads made of stone and teeth have been found in La Quina, France, dating to the dawn of the Upper Paleolithic period (about 38,000 BC), and vines, gut or sinew were probably used in their stringing. Stone implements (from which the combined Paleolithic, Mesolithic and Neolithic periods derive the general name 'the Stone Age') could also be lashed and bound to wooden shafts with the same materials, although scholars continue to debate the date at which this first occurred. Indeed, the dates of Stone Age objects are continually being reassessed in the light of new finds, more systematic archaeological practices and more precise radiocarbon dating. That said, it is known that Stone Age toolmakers grasped the significance of twisting, which increases strength by diverting part of any tensile load into lateral pressure. Twisted strands wrapped around the held portion of a tool resulted in a better grip, and this feature is maintained in many implements today. Here we meet again

3. Pom-pom and tassel ties, first used thousands of years ago, remain important elements of human and animal tribal trappings; these braided woollen examples, worn by women of Rajasthan (in India) in their hair or at their waists, incorporate valued objects such as cowrie shells and iridescent beetle thoraxes.

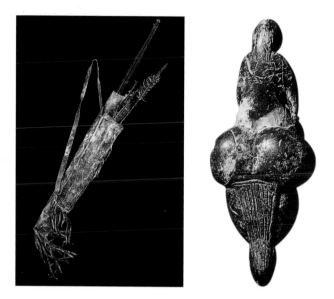

4. The importance of twisted cord for tool-making is epitomized by this Plains Indian painted and fringed hide bowcase. Twisted hide binds (or 'hafts') the stone arrow points to wooden shafts (also called 'hafts') and wraps the gripped centre area of the bow.

5. Of all garment types, skirts, loincloths and aprons composed of twisted weft extensions or added-on twisted strands have the longest history. Such a skirt is illustrated on this French Paleolithic 'Venus' figure of about 20,000 BC; actual examples have been found in sites ranging from Denmark (c. 1200 BC) to northern Arizona (AD 1000–1400) and a related form survives in the Polynesian grass skirt.

one of many words demonstrating the close relationship between textile techniques and the general development of tools: 'haft', meaning to fasten or attach, as well as meaning the handle itself.

Sinew and gut are often discounted as true fibres, but two types of evidence suggest that these were long ago subjected to the thread-making process of twisting. The first is their documented use by tribal and semi-nomadic peoples around the world; today's Samis (Laplanders) still make fine threads from twisted strands of reindeer sinew. The second is by association with the traditional treatment, especially of gut, for other uses ranging from violin and tennis racket strings to surgical sutures. Until the advent of synthetic fibres in the mid-20th century, the manufacture of catgut – usually the dried and twisted intestines of sheep, but occasionally also of horse and ass – was a thriving industry. Catgut formed the bands in lathes as well as clocks and other precision instruments, a further reminder of the importance of cordage to a broad range of human endeavour.

The earliest known cordage dates from 18,000–15,000 BC. Found in the Lascaux caves in southern France, this three-ply cord is thought to be of some type of bast fibre. Two-ply willow bast nets dated to the late 8th millennium BC have been found in Finland, and nets of linden bast from the North European Mesolithic period (c. 6000–4000 BC) have been unearthed in Lithuania and Estonia. But the fibres that became widespread are plant basts: flax and hemp (from which linen is made), and various nettles (including ramie, a native of the Far East). Varieties of one or all of these are known worldwide and examples of the first two have survived from Stone Age Europe, central Asia and Peru, although there is no substantial evidence of their use anywhere until 6000–4000 BC. These fibres are all treated in approximately the same way. The plant is dried or heated, retted (broken down by moisture, whether dew, rain or river water) and dried again. The residue of the stem-rind is then removed through breaking, flailing and finally combing the inner fibres. Tree bark fibres were obtained in a similar, but more drawn-out, manner (after retting generally being boiled with wood-ash, or lye), as were esparto fibres obtained from a leafy rush native to Spain and northern Africa (although salt water rather than fresh water is used in their retting).

Numerous plants are more obviously and immediately useful, and basket-makers around the world still manipulate these in ways especially revealing of prehistoric processes, since the craft has never been mechanized. For example, many varieties of palm tree grow in tropical and subtropical regions around the globe, and entire fronds from these, with long ribs splaying from a central spine, are today still interlaced into hats, mats, walling and bags in the Pacific and Caribbean Islands and elsewhere. Ribs (or leaflets) stripped from their spine are also worked, or, like many other appropriate materials (including bamboo, the vine-like

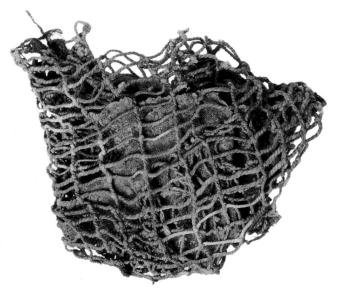

6. Knotted netting produces a robust, flexible structure suitable for many functions. Here knotted two-ply flax cords, radiocarbon dated to 390–350 BC, form a carrier for a cast metal vessel from the Tarim Basin (in modern-day Chinese Turkestan). At the earliest known New World urban centre, Caral in Peru (c. 2600 BC), large, similarly knotted reed bags filled with stones were used to form the inner walls of buildings.

7. The broad-leafed New Zealand flax, cut into strips, is plaited by the Maori to replicate a structure found naturally in palm fronds. By using the simplest interlacing or 'over–under' techniques, a range of containers can be made.

8. Standing in front of a buckskin bag decorated with sinew-sewn glass beads is a birch-bark basket with a wrapped, coiled edge and fragments of blue and red woollen shroud cloth overhand stitched with sinew. Both objects were made in the 19th century by Eastern Woodlands Indians of the Northern Maize Area (southern New England and Maryland to lower Missouri).

climbing palm, rattan, and roots, sinew and rawhide), divided into narrow strips. Split numerous times and twisted, leaf fibres such as palm, pandanus (of Panama hat fame) and New Zealand flax produce very fine threads.

Yucca and sisal fibres (natives of the southwestern United States and Latin America) must be scraped out of the pulped leaves, but many plant materials require no pre-treatment. Grass stems and reeds (both hollow like bamboo) are simply harvested and dried, while willow, hazel and other hardwood saplings, as well as rushes and all the palm-like materials, need only to be moistened to make them pliable. Bark, too, can be used as found. Elm and birch are the most common trees in the northern hemisphere with an inner layer of bark that can be pulled off in sheets. Strong, flexible and water resistant, bark sheets have been put to use in various ways by more recent hunter-gatherers. Bound around the legs they served as protective *chaparreras* among several Native American tribes, while around the world footwear is still made from stranded bark. White birch-bark canoes were so widely adopted in 19th-century northern American woodlands that canoes there were called 'birches'. And just as inhabitants of the tropics could make impromptu

9. This ochre- and pigment-painted New Guinea woman's rainhood is plaited and worked with decorative knots. It is about 50 centimetres (20 inches) long and typifies the many prehistoric artifacts easily made from a wide range of 'found' fibres that require no spinning.

food carriers from palm fronds, northern forest-dwellers discovered that pieces of bark-sheet could be softened with heat and bent into containers, held in place by a long spear-like pin (which also served as a handle).

With such abundant and self-evident sources, it may be wondered why basts – especially flax and hemp – achieved such supremacy as fibre-producing plants, since they are time-consuming to prepare and difficult to dye. Nevertheless, by 5000 BC, *Linum usitatissimum* (flax) was domesticated in parts of modern-day Iraq and Iran, and by 3000 BC it had spread southwestwards to the rest of Iraq, Syria and the Egyptian Nile, and northwestwards as far as Switzerland and Germany. In the same period hemp spread eastwards from central Asia to northern China, where, except for gut and sinew from deer, it was the principal fibre until the later introduction from the south of ramie, followed by cotton. At the same time, hemp spread northwestwards, again as far as Switzerland and Germany, where seeds have been radiocarbon dated to 5500–4500 BC. Tree basts, however, were not entirely replaced: elm, oak and linden bast fibres were found side-by-side with flax in the important Neolithic 'Swiss lakes' finds dating to 4000–2000 BC. While no textiles survive from Japan's Jōmon era (*c.* 10,000–300 BC), the braided cords preserved as impressions on Jōmon earthenware pottery are understood to have been made of fibres from wild trees and vines; hemp arrived towards the end of this era, yet tree bast and related long leaf fibres are still used in Japan today.

Flax and hemp were first grown and exploited in temperate grasslands, which offered neither the rapid growth nor the ample choice of vegetation characteristic of tropical rainforests and northern woodlands. However, both plants adapt well to a range of habitats (there are today some 230 varieties of flax) and have many uses apart from as fibres. Pressed flax seeds, for example, produce linseed oil for weatherproofing fabrics such as sailcloth and are today still a basis for painting with ochre, an iron-rich clay known by Paleolithic peoples to produce shades from red to golden yellow. The compacted seed residue likewise serves to feed ruminants such as cattle, pigs and camels. The seeds are also ground for bread, soothing poultices, tea-like infusions and, mixed with honey, a cough medicine. The flowers provide nectar for honey-bees (and wax and honey were used in many ways, including for resists and in embalming respectively). Hemp spread widely in part due to its ability to grow in dryer, poorer soil. This results in a finer fibre, which is also often

10. The variation in structural texture and scale possible with tree, vine and plant bast fibres provides much of the impact of this post-1860 central African Tshokwe mask. Its interlooped and knotted head-dress is further embellished with strung beads and couched husks. It provides but one model for the way beads may have been used in 20,000 BC.

called 'linen'. It tolerates more rigorous climates, its waste can be used as a fuel and its seeds have food value; in addition there is the long-established medicinal and spiritual use of some varieties' narcotic resins.

Several plant and tree basts also provide oils and astringents for tanning leather, and their colouring tannins are one of the few substances readily absorbed by plant fibres, all further evidence of the symbiotic relationship between the exploitation of animal carcasses and basts. Gut, sinew and basts also share other characteristics. They are strong, flexible, lustrous, relatively inelastic and, in the medium term, impervious to water. Bast fibres thus served for caulking and hemp is especially resistant to the rotting effects of salt water, hence its long association with maritime uses. Importantly, they all come from nature in lengths long enough to be useful. Silkworm gut, more than 100 metres (330 feet) long and the most elastic of this group, is used for continuous fishing line. The cocoon is soaked in acetic acid, or vinegar, after which it is split open so that the gut can be unrolled. (A northern Chinese Neolithic 'cut' cocoon is the

11. Fur and feather yarns are found as early as 10,000–8500 BC from Yucatan through Mexico to the Prehistoric Southwest. From the latter comes this AD 400–700 northern Arizonan infant's blanket, shown in detail to reveal yucca or agave threads twined around warp strands (here running horizontally) themselves plied with rabbit belly fur.

earliest sign of the awareness of silkworms, so silk gut probably preceded silk fibre, which is extracted while leaving the cocoon intact.) Flax fibres are typically 30–100 centimetres (12–40 inches) long and hemp fibres 90–250 centimetres (3–8 feet) long. All lend themselves to knotting or splicing when additional length is needed. Indeed, some tree and vine basts are too stiff to be spun and must be spliced or tied to obtain more than 3–4 metres (10–12 feet), their typical fibre length. Thus, splicing became widespread. The uses of spliced basts could vary from the production of relatively fine ancient Egyptian linen cloths (of which the earliest example, from Faiyum, dates to about 5000 BC) to the robust lashing-cords made by Maori women in modern times.

Another parallel between twisted gut and bast fibres is their shared applications. Both make excellent rope and reins, meshes and sieves, nets and snares. These are the 'working' materials essential to nomadic, herding, fishing and farming peoples alike. All the evidence suggests that these, together with reeds, grasses, sapling rods and so forth, were by far the earliest materials manipulated by humans in ways recognizable as textile techniques. And where one material was not readily available, another could serve. Such a substitution is preserved in the name for mesh-like open-weave cloths, treated with size for rigidity and composed of linen threads highly twisted for extra strength and stability: today these are called 'catgut' or 'catgut gauze' (depending on their structure) and they are used as a base cloth for embroidery. There are two useful lessons to be drawn from this example. Shifting textile terminology is commonplace and while sometimes revealing, as here, can often be misleading if taken at face value. In addition, today's 'catgut' is a reminder that Stone Age fibres and materials were best able to satisfy both practical needs and a desire for variety through structural changes (of spacing, means of interconnecting, degree of twist, fineness of fibre) or the *carrying* of colourful decorations (rather than being highly coloured themselves).

The concept of carried decoration returns the discussion to the question of how those Gravettian bands, caps or hairnets were made. When turning to structure, it is important to set aside the convenient but often confusing divisions between sewing, basketry and cloth-making, and to look instead at the common principles at work. These can be categorized into three motions: twisting, looping and interlacing. The most fundamental twisting action, for strength, has already been considered.

17

The resulting spiral of a twisted thread is 'mimicked' in the spiralling hand motion used in wrapping and one of the basic sewing stitches, an overhand stitch that reinforces or joins edges or else can be used as a decorative addition known as 'stem stitch'. The same action is used to make twined textiles. At its simplest, paired strands are twisted and then passed – one behind and one in front – around a second material; by repeating the twist-pass-twist-pass process, the secondary element is locked between the spiralling ones. Crammed one row above the other, weft-twining results in a solid but pliable surface, but the locking action means it can also be widely spaced, producing openwork structures in both baskets and cloths. In either case the technique is well suited to relatively short active elements, spliced together when more length is needed, since the spiralling strands must be manoeuvred through successive twists.

Coiling also exploits a spiralling motion, in two ways. Sapling rods, cordage or bundles of reeds, grasses, bast fibres and the like are held together by a form of wrapping or overhand sewing that takes the binding around two or more rods or, especially with bundled materials, through the preceding bundle. Plaited materials can also be coiled, either as the plaiting progresses or afterwards. All of these variations require only

12. The spiralling structure typical of both twined and coiled baskets is often emphasized by their patterns. The shallow coiled Havasupai basket, from Arizona, incorporates blackened 'devil's claw' with willow. Behind it is an Alaskan Tlingit twined split-spruce root basket decorated with false embroidery in maidenhair fern and split-stem grass. Although twining and coiling are often associated with such sculptural forms, both techniques have direct parallels in weaving, embroidery and sewing.

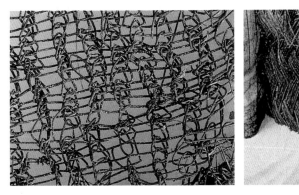

13. This detail of a 400 BC looped horsehair hairnet found in the Tarim Basin shows an overhand loop brought back from right to left through a loop two rows above. Since such a structure is secure but loose, it is often called 'knotless netting'. If some loops were pulled tightly closed, the result would be 'knotted netting'.

14. Walls and fences of tied, bundled and interlaced materials have had widespread use. This example displays two techniques, lashing and diagonal interlacing (plaiting).

needles and awls, and even these can be dispensed with if the binding material is firm enough to push between or through the coils. An arm's length of binding is as much as can be controlled easily and the core can be spliced or continuous, the latter still not implying true spinning, since many suitable materials, such as rattan, can be up to 135 metres (450 feet) long. Whatever the core, it is typically arranged in a spiral to form mats or very firm bowls and baskets, and coiled pottery most probably evolved from this technique. (The practice of lining baskets with clay is also a precursor of ceramics, which are associated with the fully evolved stages of Neolithic cultures. However, cordage wrapped around a shaped removable core and coated with asphalt or bitumen provided an equally watertight vessel. This technique itself has a long recorded history, from at least the 7th millennium BC until the early 20th century, when baskets were still being caulked by the Yokut Indians of central California.)

Spiralling constructions are associated with strength, but because twining, coiling and wrapping require two separate elements, they can be weighty. Looping techniques, which use only one element, are thus better able to produce very lightweight, flexible constructions. The basic loop is still an overhand 'stitch', worked loosely along a taut horizontal cord in the first instance and thereafter into the row above. This is called 'linking'; modern chain-link fencing is made this way. In sewing and related needle techniques an overhand stitch can be secured by being passed back around itself before going forwards again, creating a buttonhole stitch; as an independent construction the same action is termed 'knotted netting' (particularly for fishing nets and ancient hairnets) and numerous other interlooping techniques arise from it, including knitting with one or more needles. Although associated with nets such as those found in Mesolithic

15. In the fringes of this 19th- or early 20th-century AD band from Timor in Indonesia, two patterned sections of weft-twining alternate with two of warp-faced plain weave. The band is finished with beading and red cloth tassels, demonstrating how easily different techniques can be combined along the same warp threads.

northern Europe, both linking and looping can be worked very tightly: the looped sisal *shigra* of Ecuador, for example, was originally made to carry water.

Interlacing is the final motion involved in manipulating materials and is an over–under action (in sewing, a running stitch). In weaving, the weft – called the 'weaver' in basketry – alternates to an under–over course in every other row, and variations depend solely on changing this regimented passage (called 'plain' or 'tabby' weave) into a more rhythmic 'over two, under two', or 'over two, under one' and so on. Tabby is a firm, strong construction suitable for fences and walls. Plaiting is interlacing too, but usually worked on the diagonal and thus much more flexible, as is its near-relative, sprang, which is first suggested by ceramic impressions from Neolithic Germany. While netting and sprang dominate in northern Europe prior to about 3000 BC, all of the remaining techniques, with several variations, are found in surviving examples of mats, baskets, impressions or the occasional cloth from as early as the 7th millennium BC in the Middle East, about 5000 BC in Mesoamerica, and later in Peru. Twining and knotted or twisted netting predominate and none of these requires a true loom, although fine-fibred twined cloth must at least be worked on a taut warp. Twining can also be worked 'sideways', by twisting paired warps and inserting a core through them. This warp-twining is often called 'false weaving' as the results resemble woven cloth. Warp-wrapping and warp-interlooping present similar complications.

The terms 'warp' and 'weft' relate primarily to the loom: the warp is under tension and the weft is inserted across it. Thus the taut cord on which linking and looping depend might also be called a warp. Today many practitioners distinguish between 'passive' and 'active' elements to avoid such confusion. However, the behaviour of the material – rigidity versus flexibility – is the key factor. All the twisting, looping and interlacing techniques can be carried out with ease if one material (or the starting point) is sufficiently rigid; if not, tension provides the required firmness. Tension can be obtained by attaching both ends of the warp threads to fixed points, by adding weights to one end, or by pulling away from fixed ends (as hair-braiding is universally achieved). Respectively, these evolved into horizontal ground looms, warp-weighted looms and backstrap (weaver-tensioned) looms, but for narrow bands and belts their maker might easily substitute two tree trunks, a tree branch and a rock, or toes and hands (the last a method preserved in Icelandic footweaving).

16. With its basketry-covered storage jar and a harp formed like a rake – in many languages called a 'loom' – the imagery on this 2600 BC harp from Sumerian Ur (western Iran) illustrates the close relationship between textile techniques and the development of settled communities. The wolf and the lion carry food and drink; the knife for carving is tucked into the wolf's waistband. The ass plays a harp with strings quite probably made from catgut. And at the bottom left, the scorpion man is depicted as partially braided, illustrating the way in which textile techniques and their terms readily become analogies for mysteries of nature and the universe.

The first evidence of warp-weighted looms is provided by stone weights from 6000 BC found in Hungary. Other looms, being made entirely of wood and cord, have left no trace of their earliest forms. Nonetheless, representations of fully evolved Egyptian and Mesopotamian horizontal ground looms, dating to just before 3000 BC, show three rods across the warp. Two of these, the shed and heddle rods, control alternate warp threads and provide an automatic 'shed', or opening for the weft. Automatic shedding has several forms (see Chapter 2) and designates the device as a true loom. (A legacy of the importance of these rods remains in other meanings of 'loom', such as the handle of an oar or, as late as the 19th century, a rake or long-handled tool generally.) Evidence of wide-loom weaving increases after about 4000 BC and cloths themselves survive from this time in 16 northern Europe and southeastern France. Even then, the wefts are often only twice the width of the cloth, making it easy to pass them through the shed without a shuttle or to interlace, twine or wrap the warp using the fingers alone, all of which again suggest the benefits of long bast fibres, plied and spliced as needed.

Clearly, even without true spinning or true looms a vast range of textiles could be made. Among hunter-gatherer peoples who survived into the 20th century, the northern Japanese Ainu are but one example of non-spinning weavers, in their case using fine knotted strands of elm bark for thread. In addition, various inner barks of mulberry or ficus, when stripped and retted, provide textiles that are neither spun nor woven. Known as 'tapa' cloths after the term applied to those made in Polynesia, bark cloths were also widely made in central Africa, Indonesia and the Americas (especially in far northwestern zones), and from Mesoamerica down to the Andes, Amazon and Gran Chaco regions in South America. In bark cloths the glutinous sludge resulting from the retting is beaten into large, thin, supple sheets, which could be painted or stamped with readily available colourants such as ochreous earths and tannins. Ordered layers of reed-like papyrus strips, treated with a slightly longer fermentation process and then pressed together rather than beaten out, are better known as the ancient Egyptians' paper. However, papyrus and esparto – the latter still widely used in paper-making – were also used as prehistoric sources of fibres.

Both bark cloth and paper result from the chemical breakdown of a gluey non-cellulose matter from the cellulose compounds in vegetable fibres, leaving a self-adhering mash intact (instead of rinsing away all but the cellulose to obtain fibres).

17. While the indigo dyed, embroidered and appliquéd cotton cloth of this Ainu kimono represents a later tradition, the garment's principal fabric demonstrates the survival of an ancient technique in its incorporation of brown threads made from fine knotted strands of elm bark.

18. This pygmy bark cloth, about 28 x 75 centimetres (11 x 30 inches), is small compared to those of some other cultures, which can measure twice this size. For even greater size two or more cloths can be pasted together. Thin and supple, bark cloth may be deeply gathered as in the calf-length 'kilts' worn by Cameroonian men into the 20th century.

Felting, the other prehistoric method of making textiles without spinning or weaving, is in contrast a mechanical process in which scaly-surfaced wool and some other hair fibres can be adhered together into shaped or moulded sheets by a combination of moisture, heat and pressure. Wool is extremely elastic and provides excellent insulation as cloth, felt or padding. This fact clouds the discovery of compressed wool 'fabrics' in modern-day Turkey at the Anatolian plateau settlement Çatal Hüyük (6500–6000 BC), one of the earliest known caches of textiles since, as wool felts naturally, these could equally be the result of extreme post-burial pressure on wadded wool-fibre padding. Some three thousand years later the first well-documented example of felt appears, from Beycesultan, also in Anatolia. Lack of survival does not mean lack of use, and logic suggests that animal fibres were perhaps first gathered and pressed into protective clothing and tent felts among the earliest herding nomads of the steppes (which extend from the Ukraine to southwestern Siberia and are virtually treeless). There, and among the Kurdish tribes of the regions where sheep were first domesticated, felt has remained of foremost importance. It has often been remarked that felt was never independently discovered in the New World, but the wearing of felted hats by the

19. Felt is made by compressing scaly-surfaced fibres such as wool, often by rolling as is being done here by Kurdish women of Behelke Yomut in the mid-20th century. Twined matting is used not only to keep the moist felt clean but also to surround the base of the felt-covered yurt to provide ventilation.

indigenous Saraguro peoples in Andean Ecuador is regarded as a survival from long before the Inka invasions of AD 1455.

Sheep were domesticated in the uplands of northern Iraq, perhaps as early as 9000 BC. However, they did not develop truly woolly coats for another four thousand years or so, and the first unequivocal evidence for the use of wool as a fibre dates from about 4000 BC. Irrespective of the paucity of surviving examples of wool textiles, the excavated sites typically associated with early domestication of animals give ample evidence of advanced textile techniques: Jarmo (northwestern Iraq, dated to 7250–7000 BC) revealed stone spindle whorls and weave impressions; Hacılar is in the same Pamphylian area as Çatal Hüyük; Tepe Yahyā (southwestern Iran) contained woven threads dated to the 5th millennium BC (the first evidence of weaving in that region); and Jericho (Palestine) is near to the Cave of Treasure (4000–3000 BC) at Nahal Mishmar, which contained thirty-seven pieces of undyed linen and eight pieces of wool, some in different colours (red, green, black and tan). By 3500–3000 BC sheep rearing was a major industry as far southeast as Sumeria, a textile-rich Mesopotamian civilization near the Persian Gulf, and by about 3000 BC felt and other wool textiles survive from an area limited to the shorelands of the Caspian Sea and stretching across Anatolia and around the eastern Mediterranean northwest as far as modern-day Germany and Switzerland (but not Italy). In the Andes the camelid alpaca and llama were also domesticated in the pre-ceramic period; the exact date is uncertain but spun camelid fibres were used in Chilean desert coastal cultures of the 3rd millennium BC, followed by the associated development of sophisticated textiles.

Animal fibres (except those for felt) must be spun, unless they are long enough – as are the widely used human and horse hairs – to be used simply by twisting. Thus the development of true spinning – called 'draft' spinning – is associated with the use of relatively short hair fibres (those from some camels and goats can be even shorter than sheep's wool). Their preparation mirrored the final stages of bast fibre preparation: flailing and combing removed unwanted particles and aligned the fibres to produce a bundle from which draft spinning simultaneously drew out and twisted a 'brusk', firm worsted-type yarn. As with the introduction of hair fibres, the pattern of developments in spinning is uncertain. Evidence in the form of spindle whorls from the 7th millennium BC onwards can be an indication of draft spinning, but spindles are also used in twisting and plying alone

and fibres can be spun simply by rolling them down the thigh. The earliest examples of draft-spun woollen thread date only from 4000–3500 BC. Where draft-spun *bast* fibres survive among the 7th-millennium BC Çatal Hüyük textiles and many other Neolithic finds north of the Mediterranean, it has been reasoned that wool must have already been draft spun in the same areas. This makes sense at sites such as Çatal Hüyük, where sheep remains as well as the compressed wool fibres were found. Nevertheless, it does not account for the independent – and essential – development of draft spinning for cotton, cultivated in late Neolithic India and in coastal Ecuador and Peru at about the same time, nor of wild silks, about which little is known, except that spun yarns of mixed cotton and wild silk are later found in India (*c.* 1500–1000 BC). A few cotton threads radiocarbon dated to 4450–3000 BC were found in Dhuweila (in modern-day Jordan), but may have been imported via the Red Sea from India or the present-day African states of Sudan and Ethiopia, where a different variety of cotton was known.

At the very least by 4000–3000 BC thread-making was a sophisticated craft that in many regions also included the use of a distaff. It might also be inferred that sheep, goat and camelid fibres, the relative latecomers, are by 3000 BC already widely recognized for their warmth and elasticity, and the finest of bast and cotton fibres for their coolness and comfort next to the skin.

21. Seven Precolumbian Peruvian handwoven cottons illustrate the range of possible effects with plain weaves and various diameters of hand draft-spun yarns. Such yarns, with slight irregularities and some deliberate overly tight twists, help to hold the open weaves in place.

22. As typified by this Muisca mummy unearthed in a cave at Pisba (Bogota, Colombia), burials account for the survival of many early textiles, indicating their cultural importance. For the textile historian, such examples usefully show the diversity obtained through ingenious use of local materials.

What can be said with certainty is that by the later Neolithic period a complex range of materials, fibres and related technologies were in use. Nevertheless, there is still no entirely cohesive picture of the state of development, and each new find changes the outline sketch. For example, finds dated 7160–6150 BC from the Hemel Cave in the Judean desert, Palestine, include rope, netting, mats, yarns spun and plied mainly from flax, and plain (tabby) woven cloths, one dyed blue and decorated with beads and shells. These cloths are currently the earliest surviving examples, and until 1995 were thought to be preceded only by the impressions of cloth found at Jarmo. Then even earlier Upper Paleolithic impressions of plain weaves were uncovered in the Czech Republic. Thus, current knowledge of the Stone Age can only hint at the rich textile traditions that were bequeathed to the Bronze and Iron Ages, and that continued to define many nomadic and tribal peoples into our own time.

Chapter 2:   The Dye and Loom Age *c.* 3000–400 BC

The period between 3000 BC and 400 BC coincides roughly with the Bronze and Iron Ages, eras based on the evidence of metallurgical skills. Like the preceding Stone Age, these are cultural markers rather than absolute time-frames. The Chalcolithic (copper) era begins as early as 6500 BC in Anatolia, while elsewhere it precedes the working of bronze (an alloy of copper and tin) by a very short time. However, as far as skills and tools go, these centuries might better be dubbed the 'Dye and Loom Age'. Both of these innovations become better documented in this period, not only by archaeological, pictorial and written evidence (the latter appears at about this time), but also by increasing quantities of textiles surviving in places as scattered as Egypt, Switzerland and Peru. These survivals are arguably more revealing of advanced skills than other seemingly dramatic developments, such as the invention of the wheel in about 3200 BC (possibly in Sumeria), or the plough soon afterwards. An understanding of metals is also central to (and perhaps urged on by) many aspects of dyeing, and it relates to other textile processes such as the shearing of goat's hair and occasionally sheep's wool, recorded in Akkad in Mesopotamia (2300 BC). Such shears required iron, which is springy.

Iron, in the form of coloured iron oxide earths (ochres), was first exploited by Paleolithic peoples to decorate the bodies of the living and the bones of the dead. Ochres also permanently stain vegetable fibres, and even today in the Amazon basin and central Africa plant fibres are buried in coloured earth to turn them a rich brown shade. To use ochre in a purer form, the earth is placed in water and left until the heavier matter sinks; the remaining liquified clay is poured out and evaporated – just as salt is obtained from seawater – to leave the ochre pigment, which can then be ground. The antiquity and permanence of ochres are attested to by the use of a yellow variety in the cave paintings found in the Dordogne and Lot valleys in France (*c.* 40,000 BC). Significantly, the cave inhabitants not only supplemented their range of colours by using manganese oxide and charcoal blacks, but discovered that heating yellow ochre turned it red (presumably because they lacked access to the naturally occurring red iron oxide, hematite, the dominant colour in the cave paintings at Altamira, Spain, of 10,000 BC).

24

23. Despite a lack of surviving textiles, evidence of technique and use remains in other media. In scenes of spinning and weaving decorating an Attic Greek *lekythos* of about 560 BC is a warp-weighted loom showing the warp suspended from an upper beam and tensioned at the bottom with weights. Looms this wide required two weavers; here the weaver on the left is beating the most recently inserted weft upwards. See ill. 41 for the other side.

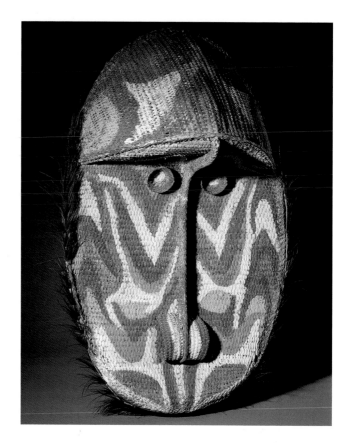

24. 'Prehistoric' colourants such as ochres and other earth pigments still form the basis of many painters' palettes; here they appear on an Iatmul plain basket-woven rattan and bushcane mask collected in Tumbanum, New Guinea, in 1950.

The processes mentioned above – using a water-based solution, grinding or macerating, and heating or boiling – together with fermentation (the retting stage in bast preparation), are the fundamental requirements for true dyeing, in which three things must happen. First, the dye matter must be extracted, usually by fermentation. Second, the fibre must accept the dye and third, it must retain it. The many dyes from roots, bark, leaves, flowers or insects are classified according to the stage at which they need assistance – respectively, insoluble, mordant and direct. These simplistic divisions disguise great complexities: dyeing often requires complex pre- and post-colouring treatments and an understanding, however intuitive, of the pH levels of the dyes, fibres and dyebaths (acid, neutral or alkali). Because animal fibres are composed of proteins, they are receptive to the acids present in most dyestuffs. The alizarin in widely known variants of the red dye-root madder will colour wool in a cold dyebath, although unmordanted the colour is pale and eventually fades.

Strong alkalis, on the other hand, destroy protein fibres, as is evident among the Swiss 'pile dweller' textiles found in alkaline conditions where only linens remained. Conversely, plant fibres are composed of cellulose and are more difficult to dye: they must be rendered acidic to take most colours, but are damaged if the acid is too strong (and so among early Bronze Age textiles found in acidic groundwater in north-central Germany, the wool in mixed-fibre cloths remained but the plant fibres had perished). As a result, dyes need to be considered in relation to the fibres suited to them.

One group of dyestuffs, all insoluble, have an affinity for any fibre. They are dissolved and deposited around fibres by reducing their oxygen content; when oxygen is reintroduced, the dye matter returns to its insoluble state, revealing its colour. Only murex shellfish dyes (often called 'Tyrian purple', although rich shades of red were also obtained) come directly from the mollusc as a whitish secretion, already reduced and photosensitive; thus it can be wiped directly onto yarns damped with seawater, as still

25. This detail of a handwoven Oaxacan *pozahuanco* (hip-wrapper) illustrates the brilliance of murex purple. The cloth is composed entirely of hand-spun cotton woven on a backstrap loom. The other colours were produced with indigo and the Latin American insect-red, cochineal. This began to be used occasionally on animal fibres in the 1st millennium BC, but only became an important cotton dye after about AD 1500.

occurs in the Oaxaca region of southwestern Mexico. Its dyestuff is nearly identical to the indican in woad and indigo; indeed, both the Solomon Islanders and Amazonian Indians discovered that chewing indigo leaves with a fruit such as lime produced a similar 'secretion' for working into or painting bark cloths. However, all three dyes – murex, indigo and woad – were used in vats by this period, the earliest archaeological evidence of which is tentatively assigned to Minoan Crete (*c.* 2500 BC).

Despite their 'any fibre' identities, indigo (found in virtually all tropical and sub-tropical regions) is far stronger than woad and in its concentrated form is dissolved in a highly alkaline solution suitable only for plant fibres. In contrast, woad (indigenous to western Asia, northern Africa and Europe) is a less potent source of dye and far less efficient in dyeing cellulose, but readily colours wools in a fermentation vat based on stale urine (for its ammonia, a mild alkali especially suited to animal fibres). Murex in a woad-type vat (pH 9, 50°C) gives a brilliant purple on wool, and cuneiform recipes pre-dating 600 BC – the earliest known – indicate that Assyrian dyers were already mixing it with an iron and tannin mordant for a near-black. Woad, which certainly *became* the blue dye for European wools (which were typically dyed in the fibre rather than the cloth), has been suggested as the colourant of the blue bast-fibre garment found at Çatal Hüyük (*c.* 6500 BC), despite the fact that the plant turnsole develops a good blue when exposed to copper, a mordant producing the greatest permanence and suited to plant rather than animal fibres. To resolve such debates requires testing, which is often hampered by the scarcity, poor condition or contamination of samples. However, there is ample evidence that dyers were aware of the beneficial or tainting effects of metal: those using traditional methods in India still prefer tin containers for red cottons but earth or clay vats for indigo. For similar reasons Persian boiling vats were made of copper or cast iron.

The extraction of shellfish purple inevitably creates mounds of used shells, the earliest of which was left by the Minoans not long after 2000 BC. In the Levant, mounds remain from about 1500–1200 BC, including some at Byblos, the important port from which the Syrians had already developed an extensive trade in sought-after textiles such as purple wool and cloth. Further south and slightly later such mounds occur at the Phoenician settlements Sidon and Tyre. Thick deposits lay in Israel, dated variously to between the 13th and 4th centuries BC. The rich bluish-purple shellfish shades were so sought after that

26. A Kashmiri depiction of hand block-printing and dyeing highlights the difference between mordant-red and indigo-blue dye vats. The former (right) is metal and heated to boiling point; the latter (bottom left) is a larger unheated clay vessel from which the cloth is repeatedly raised to develop the colour. The artist, working in AD 1850–60, depicts the printer placing a white substance on an indigo-blue cloth, but in fact the printed resist would have been positioned on the cloth before it was dyed.

imitations arose. The lichen orchil, for example, is a direct dye widely used on wool for its range of violets, shaded red by acids and blue by alkalis (as occurs on litmus paper, which it also dyes). In Egypt, where shellfish purples were not yet locally dyed, wool was dyed blue-violet with orchil macerated and fermented in stale urine. Orchil, which is native to the Levant and the Far East, is one of a number of direct dyes (today called 'basic' or 'neutral') made fast on animal fibres by the addition of an alkali or, more rarely, a neutral salt such as carbonate of soda. The latter was also used by Assyrian dyers to render turmeric a permanent golden yellow on wool.

Among the dyes in use in this period, turmeric (found in India and to the east) and safflower (a thistle native to southern Asia and the East Indies) are orange-yellow direct dyes with a special affinity for cotton, linen and silk. With little technical knowledge it can be observed that the after-treatment of plant fibres with an astringent such as the mordant alum, or an acid such as lemon juice, renders the colour more permanent and, respectively, tan or bright. Alum is also used to brighten dyes on cultivated silk, of all fibres the most receptive to dyes (the *Bombyx mori* is native to northern China, where narrow red silk bands and fabric fragments from about 3000 BC have been found). It also acts as the mordant for the less colour-receptive short-fibre wild silks from several species native to Anatolia, India, China and Japan. The most astringent vegetable substances are the tannins, also eagerly absorbed by plant fibres and of benefit to silk, which they strengthen and bulk up ('weight'). Insoluble, tannic acids are precipitated by alkalis and can be used alone for their rich tans to brownish-blacks or as a mordant for cotton and linen. Although associated with oak trees in the northern hemisphere, tannins are found in the bark and fruit of many plants, especially sumac, myrobalan (later and for centuries an important export from India), Chinese and Turkish gallnut and, in very concentrated form, in the rich brown catechu, or cutch, from several species of acacia trees native to southeastern Asia and the East Indies. Taking into account the fact that turmeric and safflower produce permanent reds in the presence of an alkali, a geographical grouping emerges based on astringents, alkalis, cotton, basts and silk, and distinguished by the importance of these colours – especially the brilliant yellows, orange-red and rose-red shades – in Indian, southern Asian and Far Eastern religious, kinship and courtly rituals. This might prompt a reconsideration of the suggestion that the late 3rd millennium BC red cotton cloth

27. In this 1991–1786 BC depiction of Egyptian Aamu people (thought to be ancestors of today's Bedouin) the Middle Kingdom painter rendered elaborate patterns with red ochre, the same substance that would have been used to colour the actual linen cloths depicted.

28. The silk and wool embroidery threads covering this hemp fabric from southern Macedonia were dyed in madder for red, carmine acid for scarlet and an indican (indigo or woad) for the blue-black and, when mixed with a yellow, the green. Both colours and motifs represent tastes that can be traced back to at least 400 BC.

found at Mohenjo–Daro in the Indus Valley (modern-day Pakistan) was dyed with madder, since the strongest variety (*Rubia tinctorum*) was not yet grown there, being indigenous to Asia Minor, Greece and the Levant.

Indigo is part of this 'alkali tradition'. As the name implies, it is closely associated with India (see Chapter 8), and although the use of indican-laden dyes emerged independently around the globe, a superior blue-dyeing expertise – increasingly evident between 3000 BC and AD 400 – may well have dispersed from or through that region. Safflower certainly spread westwards, perhaps as far as southern Europe, and was widely cultivated even where saffron was grown. Tests on the fifty or more pale yellow linen mummy wrappings from the Tomb of the Two Brothers in Egypt (*c.* 1650–1567 BC) found the former, but unmordanted. The only colourfast pieces in the same tomb were two with a deeper yellow, which proved to be a metallic oxide, iron buff, which is still made in the Middle East and India by combining fragments of iron in vinegar, itself made from tree saps. It is more difficult to locate the alum tradition. A very astringent salt (usually from aluminium and potassium), alum forms through the evaporation of seawater and is widely available. Its use became almost universal, not only in dyeing (although it makes wool fibres more difficult to manage), but also in tawing skins, sizing paper, medicine and making materials fireproof. It was later recorded that alumed madder was used to overdye indigo for another Egyptian alternative to murex. However, as far as can be discerned by looking at the red dyes, especially madder, with which alum is closely associated, the latter was not much used in the eastern Mediterranean until about 1500 BC.

Although there are traces of red-dyed fibres from earlier sites, the first two well-documented examples are a garment from the Great Death Pit among the royal tombs at Ur (*c.* 2500–2100 BC) and an Egyptian linen of the 6th Dynasty (2345–2181 BC). Neither were mordanted, instead being dyed with an iron oxide, hematite. In fact, all tested red linen dyes from the Middle Kingdom (1991–1786 BC) were found to be red ochres, as were examples from Egyptian settlements in Palestine dating as late as about 1570 BC. Only among the finds in Tutankhamon's tomb (1350 BC) and later, is the use of both alum and madder on Egyptian linens confirmed and so they seem to appear together. The importance of linen within Egyptian culture – and of the colour red in their funerary and religious rites – seems, then, to have encouraged the retention of the old brilliant red pigment

27

for linens until a suitable alternative (madder) was found. Even then, the replacement had to be imported from Palestine as a root or plant and its acceptance was not rapid, judging by the fact that the first hieroglyph for madder dates only to the 20th Dynasty (1186–1069 BC). In Mesopotamian texts, an Akkadian word for alumed wool dyed madder-red is found about 1300 BC, a time when maritime trade between Mesopotamia and the Indus Valley may well have transmitted the alum expertise. In Akkadian texts of about 1400 BC, found in Syria, madder alone appears, so in both Egypt and Syria the evidence corroborates contemporary accounts of a widespread eastern Mediterranean trade in alum begun some decades later.

Earlier Mesopotamian words for red specifically denote the insect-reds, kermesic acid and carmine acid. (India, Burma and southeastern Asia have the insect *Coccus lacca*, giving the red dye lac, as well as shellac.) At least nine varieties of the kermes insect are known. Four contain kermesic acid, of which two related kermes oak-dwellers are found in southern Europe, northern Africa and in some Middle Eastern regions, and two more are found in Israel. Carmine acid comes from the so-called 'Turkish' or 'Armenian' kermes found on grasses around Mount Ararat in eastern Turkey and the cactus-dwelling cochineal of Latin America. Three root kermes, known as 'Polish' kermes, contain both acids and are found from eastern Germany to the Ukraine, with related species in Siberia and Russia. These all dye white wools a good permanent red, but only when pre-treated with alum or, for real brilliance, tin. The tin red became known as 'scarlet'.

Since insect-reds do not take well on plant fibres, the dried kermes remains found in Neolithic layers at Adaouste, southern France, may not have produced the red found there on basts; judging from both later accounts and linguistic evidence, the secret of kermes pre-treatments still eluded western Europeans in Roman times. Like many dyes including indigo, and dyewoods such as Brazilwood, cochineal later became an important export from the Americas to Europe, yet it has been found in only three of some 150 Peruvian samples dating up to AD 100 and a handful more for the next 1,400 years. All the remainder were *Relbunium*, a close relative of the European madder-root dye. Clearly, however, some Peruvian Paracas dyers (900–200 BC) discovered the effects of tin or alum on insect-reds. That this knowledge appears not to have spread widely is typical. Recipes were carefully guarded and examples remain rare well beyond Roman

29. While *Relbunium* red dyes are typical for pre-1500 Peruvian textiles, in this Pachacamac cotton-warp slit-tapestry band of AD 1000–1350 it was cochineal that was used to dye the mainly two-ply camelid weft yarns in three colours: pink, brownish-pink and, with an iron mordant, purple-black.

times and are only for wool. Paracas dyers also used murex, and some 120 colour varieties survive, all derived from a handful of dyes including indigo and unknown sources of yellow-browns, the most abundant natural dyes.

Weavers exploited these colours to varying degrees (for printing and pattern dyeing, see Chapter 7). There were many plain cloths – that is, both plain in weave and all one colour – and in cold regions many wool cloths were subjected to a felting treatment called 'fulling'. This process of water-based nap-raising and pounding obliterated the weave and with it any irregularities or yarn weaknesses, leaving a firm dense cloth, called 'woollen', that repelled water and wind. For religious reasons there was a predominance of white wool among Jewish communities and, in Egypt, laboriously bleached linens (which from as early as 2800 BC were sometimes pleated). Even here, touches of colour appeared as border stripes or in purple wool edgings. The most extensive early group of western European textiles is that of the Swiss 'pile dwellers' (*c.* 3000 BC), whose plain linen weaves were distinguished by complex closing borders, some with interlaced and plaited fringes. These were decorated with interwoven, twined and warp-wrapped supple-mentary (and so probably coloured) weft stripes or geometric patterns, which were also created with sewn seed-beads. Knotted netting provided not only nets but flexible seam joins, and netting techniques had a long and widespread history in the north. However, the use of seed-beads and weft floats also links the Swiss weaving culture to finds of about 2000 BC in northern Italy, and the same tradition is indicated in southeastern France.

Not surprisingly there is ample evidence elsewhere that stripes were introduced down entire cloths, whether through dyed yarns, using fleece of several colours, compacting sections of warp, or juxtaposing a group of warp threads spun clockwise (S-spun) with another spun anticlockwise (Z-spun). The latter technique is associated with Scandinavia and northwestern Europe after about 1300 BC, when the presence of weights indi-cates the introduction of a warp-weighted loom for woollen weaving. (Prior to this, coarse woven cloths surviving in, and to the north of, Denmark date only from about 1800 BC and the uneven tension in several Bronze Age Mound People's kempy wool cloths suggests the use of a tubular-warp loom, which was perfectly suitable for non-elastic plant fibres.) More complex combinations of stripes and plaids with a range of twill weaves – many showing a localized colour palette of copper-red, blue and

30. A Danish belt of 1300–1000 BC illustrates how stripes form when groups of Z-spun (outer) and S-spun (inner) warps are juxtaposed in a warp-faced weave. The fringe echoes the construction of a Stone Age string skirt (see ill. 5).

31. A reconstruction of a warp-weighted loom-woven Swiss linen of about 3000 BC shows the complex patterns made possible by incorporating extra wefts; such additions, which overlie the ground cloth and do not run from selvedge to selvedge, are called 'brocading wefts'.

olive green – dominate the worsted cloths of 1000–400 BC found in Austria and associated with the Hallstatt culture. This culture extended eastwards along the Danube into Hungary, westwards into eastern France, and later spread from Spain to Britain, where the twilled plaid survived in the form of Highland tartan. In the British Isles, the earliest textile finds are Irish (750–600 BC) but these already show the use of advanced techniques, such as the earliest known examples of uneven twills, including the remains of a black horsehair sash woven in a displaced herringbone twill and elaborately fringed at both ends.

These northern and central European techniques may have been gleaned from eastern neighbours, but the only textiles surviving from eastern and central Europe from about 2500 to 1000 BC to demonstrate their transmission are a plaid found at Tsarskaja in the northwestern Caucasus (dating between 2500 and 2000 BC) and a single 3rd millennium BC twill from Anatolia. Similarly in the steppes and Hellenic Aegean (c. 2000–338 BC) little remains for much of the period, and there is virtually

nothing at all from Syria, Mesopotamia and beyond to the south and east. Written and pictorial evidence nevertheless confirms a widespread use of decorated cloth.

The addition of beads, tassels, loops and embroidery extended the possibilities for added richness. Beads of blue, white, green and yellow faience – and gold – were found at Troy in modern-day Turkey. The gold beads, dating from about 2300 BC, were found lying among loom weights, suggesting that they were strung along one weft and held in place by the next weft (just as Native American *wampum* belts were also made). Occasional finds survive over a wide area, and include garments employing large numbers of woven-in and sewn faience beads, and similarly bead-laden netted overgarments found in an Egyptian outpost (Kerma, *c.* 1800 BC) and in a dynastic centre (Tutankhamon's tomb, 1350 BC). Even more faience beads have been found at sites associated with Mycenaean Crete (1450–1300 BC), where gold platelets and gold foil-covered wooden 'sequins' have also been unearthed.

The earliest piles were attached like tassels. In the Swiss finds of around 3000 BC, piles were inserted into mats and baskets, and by the Bronze Age in northern Germany and Denmark (2000–700 BC) the practice of adding pile to cloaks and head coverings was not uncommon. A purple linen-like undergarment decorated with red pile was discovered at Tsarskaja, and at the roughly contemporary royal tombs at Ur (*c.* 2500 BC) the long threads forming a very deep pile rightly reminded the excavators of the skirts depicted on Sumerian monuments. There were two ways to create such 'false' piles: by inserting the threads between the twists while twining, as in Maori chieftain and Hawaiian feather cloaks, or by creating the same grasp through a twined embroidery stitch, which may well be the function of the stitching found both in early Bronze Age Denmark and mid-Bronze Age Jericho. At Kerma, some piles were formed from long feather-barbs, although the majority were of linen inverted U-shaped strands laid into a basket-weave cloth. The first known continuous weft-loop piles, found at Deir-el-Bahari, near Thebes, date to some two to four hundred years earlier (*c.* 2000 BC). Weft-looping covers the top of the earliest near-complete Greek garment (*c.* 1000 BC) and scraps from a northern Italian Villanovan tomb (late 9th century BC). Meanwhile, the technique continued to be exploited beyond 400 BC in Egypt, although it ceased to be used to form geometric patterns, and instead began to create a very shaggy all-over looped pile.

34

32. This late 18th- or early 19th-century Iroquois *wampum* belt is a rare example of woven beading. Over 1,000 tubular shell beads were threaded seven at a time onto the weft and secured by the returning weft, which runs alternately around each warp and through each bead.

33. The earliest surviving cloth with continuous weft-looping was made in Egypt in around 2000 BC; this example was made there some 2,500 years later. The inset purple wool tapestry band reflects Roman tastes, and may have been dyed with orchil, murex or madder mordanted with iron.

Many twining techniques were ultimately to become highly developed by the Maoris, Peruvians, Mesoamericans (where the loom is recorded after 1800 BC) and North American tribes, who used them as means of attaching feathers and the like to a wide range of objects. Yarns twined around fur fibres are particularly associated with North America's Prehistoric Southwest. In the Cueva de los Murciélagos finds in Andalucia, Spain (*c.* 3000 BC), several twining techniques – as well as some plaiting and weaving – were used in baskets, sandals, bags, caps, a necklace and a full tunic, all made of esparto. In contrast, by the Spanish Bronze Age (*c.* 1200–800 BC) the finds predominantly are of fine and regularly woven plain weaves of flax and other plant fibres. This transition is so entirely in favour of weaving that it suggests the introduction of a heddle rod (a bar-and-loop device allowing selected warps to be lifted simultaneously). Such a shift would also indicate a growing demand for 'commercial' weaving, and certainly this is witnessed not only by surviving textiles but also by written records.

34. (opposite) Bright plumage is secured with a twining stitch over the entire ground of this large cotton panel (143 centimetres or 56 inches high) made by the Peruvian Nazca between 200 BC and AD 200.

35. Quail feathers and red wool tassels were inserted under the coiled material of this late 19th- or early 20th-century seed jar, made in the Californian Tehachapi mountains by the Aztecan people of Tejon, the Kawaiisu.

36. In a tomb model of an Egyptian linen-weaving workshop of 1850–1786 BC, the two top weavers are working a horizontal ground loom with a rigid heddle (the central rod) while another (right) prepares a warp and the fourth (bottom left) holds a spindle full of spliced flax yarns.

37. The prominent horizontal ribs in this Danish Bronze Age sprang hairnet indicate where one rod would have been inserted to temporarily secure previous twists in the vertical strands while the next twist was made.

38. (opposite) This backstrap loom illustrates features common to all heddle looms. The heddle rod (c) is secured by loops to certain warps (k) to raise them simultaneously; this action overrides the shed rod (b), which creates the natural shed, or opening, for the weft or bobbin (l, e). Plain or tabby weave is shown; additional heddles or shed rods create more complex weaves. The top rod (a) is secured to a post or tree, and tensioned by the weaver who leans back against the tied-on strap. The stick or 'sword' (d) is used by the weaver to beat down the inserted weft.

Rods or shed sticks account for much that is innovative in this period. Weft loops are made during weaving by spiralling the weft over a rod laid on the cloth and then extracted. While making sprang, rods hold each successive twist until the next is in place; this is a widespread technique with early examples surviving in Denmark (*c.* 1400 BC) and Peru (*c.* 1100 BC). Rods were also used to hold up hand-selected warps in 'pick-up' (undershot) patterns (as seen impressed on Chinese bronzes). Additional heddle rods were also required for complex weaves such as the Hallstatt supplementary weft four-end twills, Irish three-end twills and the gauze weaves of Peru (where heddle looms became highly developed in the 2nd millennium BC). Narrow items such as the heading bands needed for warp-weighted looms were still often worked using fingers rather than rods, which instead acted as *aides mémoire* in complex patterns. Textiles surviving from

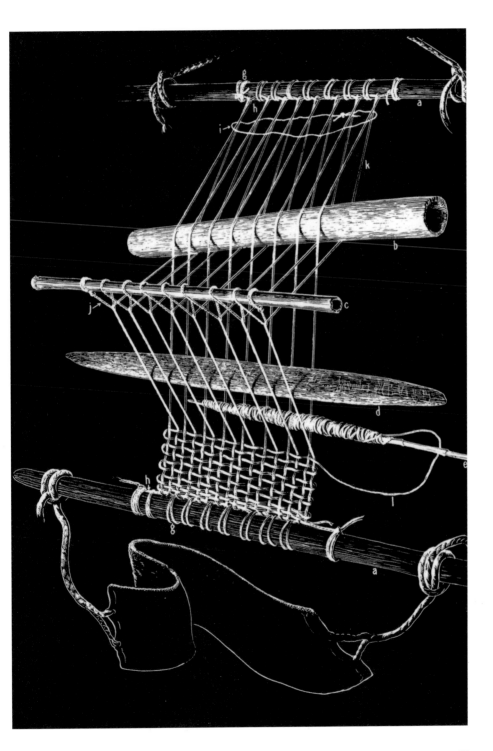

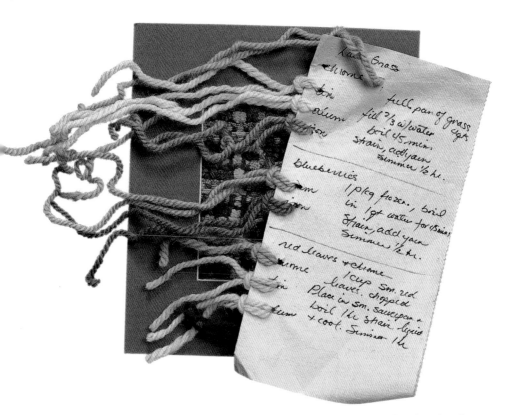

39. Three fragments of tapestry weave indicate the range of effects determined by the diameter of the warp and variations in weave structure. From top: fine Kashmiri cashmere twill-tapestry, about AD 1820; Egyptian linen warp, wool and linen weft interlocked tapestry, AD 400; coarse Peruvian cotton warp, camelid weft slit-tapestry, AD 1000–1500.

40. The brightening effect of a tin mordant is apparent in these woollen yarns dyed with easily found sources such as lawn grass, shown treated with (from top) mordants of chrome, tin, alum and iron; the red yarn was dyed with murex. Behind is an example of 'cloth cross-dyeing' with one dye on different-fibre yarns.

Swiss, Caucasus and Hallstatt cultures indicate that these bands – always warp-faced – were anyway woven with threaded tablets which, when rotated, automatically form sheds by raising or depressing warps (usually four, one through each corner).

There remained, then, a high proportion of finger-worked techniques such as braiding, twining, wrapping, sprang and tablet weaving. In loom weaving it is also possible to inlay pattern, that is, to hand-manipulate wefts to fill only the area where they are needed, rather than running from selvedge to selvedge or being a brocaded addition. This inlaid tapestry technique is evident in Egypt around 1400–1330 BC. The surrounding cloth remained plain-woven linen, but the inserted imagery was coloured wool. This innovation (like chain-stitch embroidery) is thought to have arrived with Hyksos settlers or later workers such as the Syrians captured by Thutmose III near the end of his reign (c. 1504–1450 BC), or from similarly conquered Palestine, where the warp-weighted loom was known in the same period. This loom's orientation may have inspired the Egyptian tapestry loom, essentially a horizontal ground loom turned upright.

47

Certainly, at about the same time, the multicoloured tablet-woven bands that usually accompany warp-weighted weaving (being used to form the top band) appear in Egypt, but apparently on their own.

Evidence of the exchange of cloth, skills or workers themselves increases after about 1500 BC, as both trade and expansionist cultures left their mark. As early as about 1700 BC the Phoenicians traded in dyed wool, but it was for their domination of the murex market throughout the 1st millennium BC that they were famed. They sailed to the Atlantic shores of Africa and Spain in search of shellfish, at the same time selling wool, cheaper dyes, dyed cloths and other textiles. The esteem that kermes attracted induced the Anatolians to trade their gold and silver to obtain Assyrian tin (for mordanting) as well as textiles, while the Phoenicians obtained tin in Spain and possibly as far away as Britain. But the period from about 1300 to 600 BC was also one of displacement and cultural diffusion, during which Mycenaean Greece collapsed and gradually entered a 'dark age'. After about 800 BC, Greek colonization advanced, thus spreading murex dyeing up the Adriatic coast and into southern Italy and Sicily. In about 1200 BC the alliances between Egypt, the Babylonians and the Hittites (who dominated much of Anatolia and Syria from around 1475 BC) collapsed. Egypt, which had extended its influence into African Nubia, entered its own four-hundred-year-long 'dark age' in 1075 BC; it was invaded by the Libyans in the north and the Nubians in the south, only to be reunited much later by more invaders, the African Kushites.

While Egyptian culture and skills were assimilated by their invaders, for much of the period between the 9th and 7th

41. Yarn preparation and spinning are shown in this drawing of a Greek *lekythos* (see ill. 23 for the other side). The figure second from the right holds a distaff from which she is draft spinning with a drop spindle. Such skills were among the textile techniques that spread with Greek colonization.

40

centuries BC the northern Mesopotamian Assyrians waged destructive wars across the Middle East, ultimately extending their control over southern Mesopotamia as far as Syria and south along the Mediterranean as far into Egypt as Thebes. The Assyrians in turn were defeated in 612 BC by the Babylonians and Medes, paving the way for the rise of the Persians (of present-day Iran) who, like the Hittites before them, originated in central Europe and the Caucasus. Expansive but benevolent, by 513 BC the Persian rulers sheltered disparate cultures in the first of the great empires, stretching from Macedonia in the west to Uzbekistan in the north and from the Indus Valley in the east to the former Assyrian strongholds in the south. Despite their ongoing and unsuccessful attempts to control the Greek Peninsula (499–479 BC), the Persians were able to restore and maintain peace within their own empire. Greece, in contrast, expanded around the western Mediterranean, but was plagued by almost constant internal warfare between 421 and 338 BC. Few textiles survived such destruction and upheaval. Nevertheless, their legacy can be discerned in their newly found importance as objects of barter, exchange, tribute and trade.

Chapter 3:   Trade and Trends 750 BC to AD 600

Not long after the beginning of the two-hundred-year period of expansion by the Greeks (*c.* 750 BC) and the reunification of Egypt (*c.* 730 BC), the first coinage came into use in Anatolia (*c.* 700–640 BC). Although archaeological evidence of trade remains from as early as the 7th millennium BC, in the period covered by this chapter it becomes the prime motive for the territorial conquests that now engulf much of the known world. Textiles were already important trade goods, but in several areas their production and distribution now make a clear and decisive shift from the opportunistic to the speculative: that is, they were made or acquired with the expectation of future distribution rather than for an immediate need. Coinage spread slowly and even where it was used, textiles typically still served as currency. Although they continue to offer important evidence of evolving human skills throughout the period, this chapter considers textiles in more detail as objects of exchange, valued for their buying (or persuasive) power, their status and their aesthetic and physical content.

Relatively scant evidence from before 750 BC clearly indicates that by 2000–1650 BC there was already an emerging pattern of textile trade, with its hub in the eastern Mediterranean, from the Levant northwards into southern Anatolia. Texts dating to the 3rd millennium BC from Elba (Syria) record textile trade with both Palestine and southern Mesopotamia, where by 2000 BC raw materials from the Indus Valley were also in circulation (having been traded for cloths from Ur). By this time, however, the Syrians had competition from the northern Mesopotamians – the Assyrians – whose merchants were already established in southern Anatolia, at Kanesh (Kultepe). It seems that the riches on offer there led to greed, suicidal warfare and, ultimately, destruction, as by around 1800 BC most Anatolian settlements lay in rubble. Out of this chaos emerged the Hittites, who gradually gained control of much of Anatolia and Syria, and advanced into Mesopotamia as far as Babylon (which they looted in around 1595 BC but never controlled). At the height of its power (*c.* 1475–1200 BC) the Hittite culture dominated a key corner of the eastern Mediterranean and sustained well-defined groups of weavers and dyers, who in turn were supported internally by travelling merchants.

42. The westwards trade in Chinese silk threads and finished cloths had reached as far as modern-day Germany by about 600 BC; some 700 years later in Classical Rome their price equalled that of gold. In this embroidered sleeve found in the tomb of a woman at Mashan, Jiangling (340–278 BC), the silk was woven into a gauze, a complex weave structure in use in China by 1500–1000 BC.

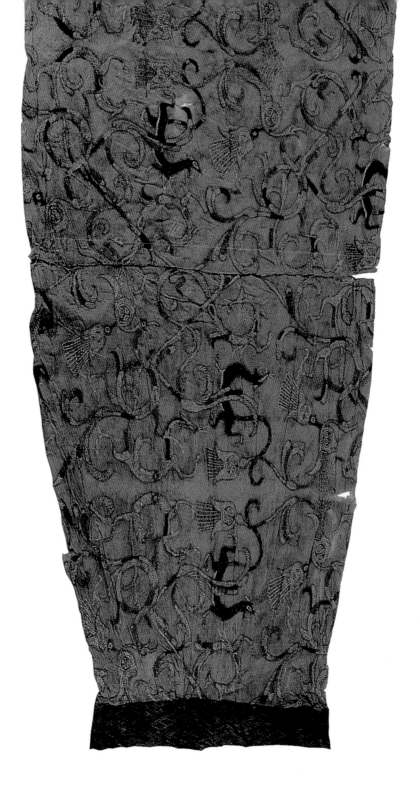

43. The scene of Dionysus in a boat on the interior of an Attic black-figured *kylix* of about 540 BC stands as a reminder both of the lasting significance of sea trade for textiles and of the importance of maritime textiles, especially hempen sails and rigging.

Meanwhile, Ugarit, Tyre, Byblos and Sidon – all in modern-day Syria but the latter three at that time Phoenician cities – were growing in importance as international trading ports. Ugarit had contact with Mesopotamia, southern Syria, Palestine, Egypt, Cyprus and Crete, and indirectly acquired raw materials, including the tin essential to scarlet wools, from as far east as modern-day Afghanistan. Often acting as 'middle men', Ugariti ships probably facilitated the textile trade between the Levant, Egypt and Minoan Crete begun in about 1650 BC. Certainly the adventurous seafaring Phoenicians did so for the Israelis, especially during the 10th-century BC reign of King Solomon (who had Phoenician assistance when developing the Israeli fleets that traded along the Red Sea). The Syrian port traders, having gained full independence with the fall of the Hittite and Egyptian empires around 1200 BC, were of such commercial significance that they remained free even after the conquest by the Assyrians (858–824 BC). The Assyrians in turn reaped many benefits from this trade in luxury goods, taking scarlet cloths as tribute and consolidating their expansion with the establishment of caravan routes and *caravanserai* (inns).

44. The imagery in this fragment of Syrian linen and wool weft-faced cloth of AD 200–300 was created with patterning heddles. The hunting scenes are small in scale, repeating vertically three times in the space of 20 centimetres (8 inches).

In central and western Anatolia, the vacuum left by the fall of the Hittites was filled by Thracian migrants from the northern shores of the Aegean, who established the Phrygian kingdom with its capital at Gordium. This kingdom was, in turn, conquered in about 700 BC by the Lydians, a western coastal Anatolian culture with a capital just inland at Sardis. A group of both decorative and utilitarian textiles from late 8th-century BC Gordium attests to the wide variety of techniques and materials made or available in the region: coloured stripes and checks, soumak, weft loops, slit tapestry and bands with compound warp-faced patterns in murex-dyed purplish-red wool and off-white vegetable fibres, their structure suggesting the use of a more advanced loom with patterning heddles of string. Simpler cloths included coverlets either of wool felted over base cloths or of a felt made of yarns laid in one direction and then the other, as papyrus paper is made. Alongside plain-woven cloths of flax and wool were those of mohair and possibly of hemp.

In many ways these parallel the limited finds from Syria. There, evidence of patterning heddles appears in the form of

45. The softly draped Greek *peplos*, as rendered in marble on a *kore* of about 520 BC, consisted of a large rectangle of fine wool woven on a warp-weighted loom. While the decorative border is part of the cloth, the small 'powdered' motifs may have been embroidered additions.

three-end weft-faced weaves, both in tapestry and, from about AD 200, in silks. The well-established trade in fine Egyptian linens at Damascus was recorded in the Book of Ezekiel (6th century BC). These linens were sold alongside sheep and goats from Arabia and white wool from Hebron, prized both in its own right and because it gave the most vibrant colours when dyed. Through this trade Syria appears to have maintained its role as a vessel for ideas; certainly by 404–343 BC the compound warp-faced patterned bands seen at Gordium were being woven in Egypt (although entirely of flax).

Syria and Anatolia, already renowned for textiles, were credited with many innovations in this period. The Roman historian Pliny the Elder (AD 23–79) recorded that the Phrygians were the originators of embroidery, although in truth only one specific technique (the use of metal thread) can be attributed to this region. The earliest example of this (*c.* 1800 BC) comes from Anatolia, where pure gold wire was used to secure dark blue faience beads. While no metal embroidery of the Phrygian period has been found to date, the examples of gold beads, platelets and sequins seen earlier came either from this area or those with which it traded. In addition, extensive Anatolian trading links with Etruscan Tuscany (750–509 BC) suggest that Tuscan finds – a gold hairnet and a disintegrated waist-to-toe garment interworked in silver and decorated with amber, faience and beads, and a purple linen cloth mixed with gold – may well have come from Phrygia. Its great mineral wealth was epitomized by one of its kings, Midas, and it was in Phrygia that coins were first minted. The legendary wealth of the last native Lydian king, Croesus (whose rule between 560 and 546 BC extended Anatolia eastwards), determined that he was the first to be invaded by the Persians, who established a garrison at Sardis. Lydia traded with the large number of Greek colonies on the Anatolian coast, all of which were allied to Attica, the area surrounding Athens. Through the control of these colonies the Persians made their first direct contact with the Greeks, with whom they continued their established trade. This trade probably accounts for the discovery in Attica of a 4th century BC linen cloth, embroidered with a diaper interspersed with tiny rampant lions of gold and silver metal threads wrapped around a fibre core. The Athenians themselves were disdainful of such ostentatious clothing, and particularly that from Macedonia, which was now the north-westernmost culture within the Persian empire. The much simpler Greek attire is often depicted on sculpture and vases

46, 47. The *shabrak* dating to about 400 BC found in Kurgan 5 at Pazyryk in the Altai Mountains (above left) incorporates metal platelets and was assembled from wool tapestries; the smaller pattern – with a kermes dyed ground, now much discoloured – corresponds to that worn by the left-hand Persian archer from contemporary Susa (above right), confirming trade between these two distant regions.

of the 6th- and 5th-centuries BC, as, occasionally, are the warp-weighted looms showing the decoration normally limited to the starting borders.

The Persian empire (550–334 BC) at its peak was roughly the size of the continental United States and equally mercantile in its focus. To facilitate trade it built the Royal Road, the first great highway, which spanned some 2,700 kilometres (1,700 miles). Starting at the Greek–Anatolian coastal colony of Ephesus, it ran past Syria and ended in Susa, just east of Ur (western Iran), which was itself at the heart of an empire stretching as far again to the east, into the western slopes of the Hindu Kush. In this context, it is easy to see how metal ornamentation and weft-faced interlocked and slit tapestries (all associated with Anatolia and Syria) could have travelled across the Persian empire ultimately to be interred among the Pazyryk Scythian burial kurgans (500–400 BC) in the Altai Mountains. The kurgans

48. Although the earliest evidence of felt may come from the site at Çatal Hüyük (c. 6000 BC), more certain examples appear much later; the most spectacular are those found at Pazyryk, which include this felt *shabrak* of about 500 BC.

contained gold-covered wooden buttons, metal platelets, patterns composed of sewn and applied beads and pyrite crystals, and the first evidence of true metallic embroidery: belts stitched along their edges with sinew thread wrapped in strips of tinfoil.

The Pazyryk burials included many items that would typify central Asian and eastern European textiles for many centuries to come: shirts of white hemp sewn together with twisted sinew, the seams and edges characteristically embellished and reinforced with red wool stitching and applied braid; felt and leather appliquéd to cloth, felt, leather and fur; and an abundance of plain and four-end twill wool cloths, mainly dyed red. The embroidery found there is largely geometric, consisting of rosettes, twill-like chevrons and lozenges of the sort that could still be found from Pakistan to Russia well over two thousand years later. Yet there were also unexpected finds, among them a brown woollen cloth with rows of weft-loop pile as seen in Gordium and earlier in Egypt, with long loops left in some rows and cut open in others. Most famously, Kurgan 5 contained a predominantly dark red carpet with a knotted wool pile, its border ringed with mounted riders and the centre a chequerboard of rosettes. Opinions based 49 on stylistic judgments are divided regarding its origins, but given the presence of metallic embroidery it is tempting to suggest the Lydians, successors to the Phrygian fame for embroidery and additionally renowned for their pile carpets. The same kurgan contained a *shabrak* of felt, appliquéd with cut up pieces of woollen tapestry, their cherry-red, kermes-dyed grounds incorporating imagery that finds parallels in Neo-Assyrian and Persian art, indicating transmission along the 46, 47 Royal Road and northwards through the Tarim Basin.

Yet even at this early date there were other ways into the interior. One followed the expansion of Greek trading colonies, thriving around the shores of the Black Sea by the 7th century BC, and providing along its upper shores contact with Scythian horseriders. There, among the 'Seven Brothers' cluster of kurgans, were found not only painted wool cloths (430–325 BC), but also tell-tale cherry-red ground tapestry (*c.* 325 BC) with the design (in this case including ducks and stag heads) worked in three colours as at Pazyryk: off-white, green (tan in the Altai), and blue-black. Another burial mound nearby (*c.* 350 BC) contained purplish-red woollen cloth embroidered in the same three colours, giving a glimpse of a taste shared among interior nomads and, perhaps, one that emanated from the original trading centres of the eastern Mediterranean, where red, yellow, green and blue was certainly a combination typical of cloths some six hundred years later. At Pazyryk there were also Chinese silks, figure-woven and plain, including one decorated in chain-stitch embroidery. Tastes and techniques were already being disseminated by a lucrative East–West textile trade.

The earliest known silk threads in the West were found among fabrics retrieved from three Hallstatt graves (600–500 BC) in Hohmichele, Hochdorf, and the Baden-Württenberg region, all in modern-day southwestern Germany. The threads are incorporated as stripes or supplementary wefts in woven cloths or used for fine embroidery, all in local styles and accompanied by other complex fabrics associated with the Hallstatts such as elaborate tablet-woven borders and complex twills. These are taken as evidence of a 6th-century BC Scythian trade route running through the interior from China to eastern Europe. It is also said that by the time of Imperial Rome (27 BC to AD 476) the unravelling of Chinese silks and reweaving in indigenous fashion was a sizeable industry. However, this is both

49. Among the textiles preserved in the frozen tombs of southern Siberia were pile carpets and fragments dating from the 6th and 5th centuries BC. This one, from Pazyryk's Kurgan 5, has one row of symmetrical or Turkish knots for three or so rows of plain-woven ground.

difficult to do and, more importantly, discounts the fact that there were by then nearer sources of silk threads. These included western Anatolia, which had an indigenous silkworm population, and the nearby Aegean island of Cos, where Pliny recorded sericulture and silk weaving had been invented.

A Roman soldier turned encyclopaedist, Pliny's opinions reflected the accepted facts and prevailing folklore of the 1st century AD. His view was distanced by both geography and time from China and the great Persian empire. Most of the latter had been conquered in 326 BC by the Macedonian Alexander the

50. With the defeat of the Persian king Darius in 333 BC, Alexander the Great laid the foundations of the Hellenistic world, in which textiles were traded from the Mediterranean to China along the Silk Route. In this mosaic depiction from 1st century AD Pompeii (based on a Hellenistic painting), Alexander wears armour made from twined and knotted leather rectangles.

Great, who united it with Greece (which his father, Philip II, had conquered shortly before). This had an immediate and lasting effect on trade and textiles. Much of Tyre was destroyed by Alexander in the process, but the gold, silver and luxurious textiles captured from the Persians helped to finance more roads, new cities and harbour developments, all supervised by Greeks and Macedonians. They introduced their language, coinage and way of life as far to the south as the Indus Valley and as far to the east as Lou-lan, at the Chinese end of the Tarim Basin. Following Alexander's death in 323 BC this so-called Hellenistic world was divided into six domains. Two of these monarchies, the Ptolemaic (whose rule included Egypt, Macedonia, Thrace and Crete) and the Seleucid (southern Anatolia and eastwards), traded as far afield as sub-Saharan Africa, Arabia and India. Caravan trails criss-crossed modern-day Iran, connecting the several roads to China that together became known as the Silk Route. Control of passage was lucrative and hotly contested. Only luxury goods were transported: wine, olive oil, metal weapons and fine wool textiles went eastwards in exchange for

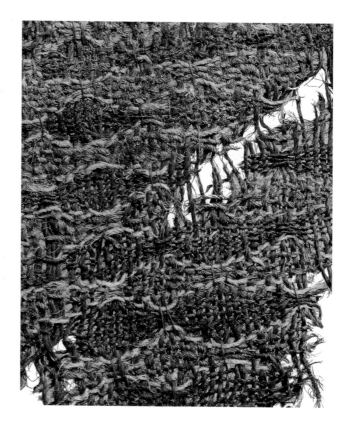

51. The weaving techniques dispersed through the movement over vast distances of both textiles and artisans include those employing distorted wefts; in this example of around 400 BC found in the Tarim Basin, the cream wefts undulate together where fewer warp intersections occur.

tea, spices and silks coming westwards. Once the latter arrived at Hellenistic ports, Greek merchants took the goods on to Greece, Italy and Spain, hence Pliny's belief that such things originated along the shores of the Aegean. The Romans, meanwhile, had united Italy in 290 BC and by 146 BC had conquered much of the Mediterranean. They destroyed Carthage (the Phoenician northern African port that had for centuries dominated textile trade along western Mediterranean shores) and forced Spain to pay a sizable tribute, half of which was in kermes.

The result was a subtle but significant change in perceptions, reflected by Pliny and holding sway well into our own time: the 'civilized' world was moving westwards. Beyond Anatolia, Syria and Judaea – the easternmost extent of Roman control – now lay in the exotic 'orient', tempting in its riches but mysterious and even decadent. It is telling that when Anthony was branded a traitor in 33 BC, he was accused of lingering with Cleopatra amid the luxuries of the eastern Mediterranean. Egypt was soon absorbed by the Roman empire, yet the profits of the textile

52. Among the most prized textiles between 750 BC and AD 600 and beyond were those of silk and gold thread; they were combined in this fragment of figured inlaid tapestry found in a Roman grave in Syria dated to AD 220. Additional expense had been lavished on the purple dye for the dark colour: weight for weight the cost of kermes and murex often exceeded that of gold.

trade and the tastes it had created were not so easily vanquished. Despite the increasing Roman admiration for, and adaptation of, all things Greek, it was the 'vulgar' Macedonian style that held sway. It was a gradual transition, represented at the inception of the Hellenistic world by the burial garments of Philip II (d. 330 BC), who lay in gold casket cloaked in plain-woven wool cloth dyed shellfish purple and enriched with tapestry depicting scrolls and mythological creatures in gold metal thread. The discreet touches of purple once worn by the Greeks were adopted by Romans as a sign of imperial approval, but soon became more extravagant. By AD 220 once-kingly attire was being used in a

53. This child's wool sock from Oxyrhyncus, Egypt, was made in the 2nd century AD by cross-loop knitting, a single-needle technique also seen among roughly contemporary Roman and Scandinavian finds and also known as cross-knit looping.

provincial Roman burial in Syria, not only with gold-thread tapestry but now also inlaid into purple silk rather than wool. When the Edict of Diocletian (AD 300–301) fixed prices throughout the Roman empire for common goods, by far the most expensive cloths were those dyed with murex, followed by those dyed with kermes scarlet.

As trade and industry flourished, so too did the development of luxury textiles, including their raw materials. Wool, for example, already the principal fibre of northern Europe by 700 BC, was enhanced by selective breeding. Subsequently, large quantities were exported as woven cloth to the southern regions from Roman Gaul (which extended from the Alps and the Rhine to the Atlantic shores of modern-day France). Good wool was in high demand. The finest of 'oriental' wools – cashmere – was to be found woven in Syria at the latest by AD 200. In Ptolemaic Egypt, sheep had been imported to improve local stock and cotton was also introduced, although the country's chief products remained linen and papyrus paper. Dyed wools there were primarily reserved for cross-looped knitting, sprang and the wefts in inlaid tapestry, the latter displaying both Greco–Roman and, from the 1st century AD, Christian Coptic imagery. Although coinage had been introduced, payments to weavers were still often made in the form of cloth or garments; these and home-produced cloths could be used to pay debts, barter or obtain slaves, which were common in all cultures throughout this period and sometimes included weavers among them.

Throughout Europe in the 1st millennium AD, records indicate widespread farm and convent warp-weighted loom production of large rectangles of coarse wool, usually with their dimensions regulated by law in order to be used as standard currency. However, in the 1st century AD the upright frame loom

54, 55. Tablet-woven items such as this Norwegian wool band of about AD 500 (shown with a reproduction, left) were used to reinforce edges and seams, as decorative additions and for many practical purposes. Such bands are found as far to the southeast as Egypt and the Caucasus.

56. The earliest known completely intact burial in China is the woman's tomb at Mashan, Jiangling, dated to between 340 and 278 BC. The body was wrapped in thirty-five items, including silk clothing (see ill. 42) and shroud cloths with an outer shroud, seen here, of brocaded silk tied with bands brocaded in a different pattern. Viewed sideways (the warp here is shown running horizontally), it is possible to discern dragon, dancer and phoenix motifs.

had been introduced, facilitating tapestry and weft-wrapping techniques. Worsted twills grew more decorative and by the final decades of the Western Roman Empire (AD 410–76) gold-brocaded tablet-woven bands and sumptuous silk and gold embroidery are found, while Frankish and Anglo-Saxon royal tombs of the 5th to 9th centuries AD reveal a growing taste for Coptic tapestries, pile carpets and Byzantine silks. The latter are named after the Eastern Roman Empire's capital, Byzantium (later Constantinople, modern-day Istanbul), which was re-established by Constantine in AD 324, some two decades after the division of the empire. Until the 7th century, the finest silks were made in imperial workshops in the capital, in provincial centres in Egypt and Syria, and, from AD 500–600, in a handful of private workshops in, for example, Tyre and Beirut. Such prestigious production aside, it remains difficult to develop a balanced picture of Western textiles in this period.

In the Far East it is a different story, and finds dating to the Southern Zhou (474–221 BC) and Han (206 BC to AD 220) Dynasties now constitute by far the largest body of textiles from this period anywhere around the globe. They can be divided into three basic types. The first and largest consists of plain cloths, including silk taffetas, made and used by Chinese peasants to pay their taxes. The second type is utilitarian – shoes, cords, sturdy cloths and so on – found both in old China and what is now the Xinjiang region (Chinese Turkestan), the northwestern frontier territory that encompasses central Asia's Tarim Basin, traversed by silk trading routes and controlled by China inter-mittently from 221 BC. The third type comprises elaborate, more widely published, cloths. Among these are spectacular embroi-dered, painted and loom-patterned silks and gauzes from sites such as the woman's tomb at Mashan, Jiangling (340–278 BC) and the Han tombs at Mawangdui, Changsha (170–140 BC), where warp loops, cut to form a pile, provided a probable proto-type for velvet weaving. In general, the weaves are warp-faced, exploiting the length and strength of Chinese silk threads. Subtle patterns repeating along the horizontal axis indicate the use of either a kind of pattern loom or multiple shed swords.

Some weft-faced fabrics have also been found, sparking the debate about the origins of Chinese tapestry techniques. Woollen tapestry (*kemao*) is not unusual in Han Dynasty and later China, but in the Tarim Basin appears as early as 400 BC in the form of narrow bands incorporated into garments made by stitching together strips of twilled, plaited and complex cloths.

57. The narrow width of many textiles of this period – from 2.5 centimetres (1 inch) to 50 centimetres (20 inches) – meant that garments were often composed of multiple lengths. In this Tarim Basin wool fragment of about 400 BC, narrow plaited bands join the texture-woven cloth to a slit tapestry band.

The same settlements provide striking evidence of the movement of cloth, people and ideas: Buddhism and indigo resist-dyed cottons from India, Hellenistic iconography in textiles at Lou-lan, Scythian imagery, Mongolian bones and parallels with finds at Pazyryk. Madder was introduced and cultivated, and from the east came two yellow Chinese grass dyes. All this might suggest that the Far East was indebted to a westwards culture for its tapestry technique. However, it has also been hypothesized that the Zhou silk weavers were already capable of weaving silk tapestry, *kesi* (presently dating only from the Six Dynasties period, AD 420–589), because they could weave much more complex weft-faced silken bands, *tao*. But in textiles the complex often *precedes* the simpler, just as 'over engineering' is often found in early architecture. Slower can be better: time-consuming skills honoured within an extended family or royal workshop only lose their currency when divorced from this environment. Furthermore, any 'doing' to provide beyond the necessities of daily or court life indicates a form of proto-industrialization. This process typically seeks to make production faster and more standardized, which generally means simpler technically – though not necessarily aesthetically.

Chinese textiles show all the signs of commercial production. About fifty thousand cocoons must be reeled to produce enough threads for 1 kilo (35 ounces) of silk; these must then be twisted together, a process aided by the development of the spindle wheel during the Zhou Dynasties (*c.* 1050–221 BC), first applied to bast fibres and then adapted for silk. Since silk is twisted ('thrown') but not spun, this was probably not a true spinning wheel, the invention of which is attributed to India (500 BC to AD 700) where it was essential for spinning cotton and wild silk. At an early point the treadle loom was developed, allowing the heddle bars to be controlled by foot pedals, freeing the weaver's hands for speedier work. With the unification of China in 221 BC, the Qin Dynasty standardized weights, measures, coinage and writing, and widths of imperial silks became fixed at 50–63 centimetres (20–25 inches) depending on their construction. Dyes and labour were often conserved by using a weft of silk left in its natural state, not degummed. Finally, the drawloom (see Chapter 4) was introduced in the 6th–7th centuries AD, possibly from Syria, although this remains open to speculation.

China also gives an insight into the mechanisms at work in the Byzantine empire and elsewhere for centuries to come. Textile tributes, in the form of garments as well as cloth, played

58. Requiring several heddle rods or shed swords, up to about AD 600 gauze weaves were associated with Peru (where they are found as early as the 9th century BC in Chavin sites) and with greater China. Their characteristic crossed warps are clearly visible in this detail of a fragment of a triple lozenge patterned Han Dynasty (206 BC to AD 220) silk unearthed at Noin-ula in northern Mongolia.

59. The dry climate of Peru's coast has preserved large quantities of textiles that would not have survived elsewhere. Among these are many large Paracas camelid mantles embellished with stem-stitched figures such as that seen here, thought to be from the Cabeza Larga necropolis (200–100 BC). A single mantle was the work of several embroiderers, who used needles of pierced cactus thorns. Collection David Bernstein, New York.

an important role in the expansion and protection of territory – gifts to the cooperative, bribes to the hostile. External trade was a royal prerogative; royal residences thus promoted international merchanting, continuing a trend apparent hundreds of years earlier in Mycenaean Greece (1600–1200 BC). Those who journeyed along the Silk Route gained useful information about competitors, as did the 7th-century AD Chinese traveller Hsuan-Tsang, who noted in Persia silks at least twice as wide as those of his own country. This mild form of industrial espionage was reinforced by artisans themselves: weavers were analysing competitors' weave structures in order to imitate them long before scholars were doing the same to understand them.

The distinction between warp- and weft-patterning is crucial to the understanding of loom developments and cloth structures – subjects that have exercised many historians. For general purposes, however, it is the appearance of the same textile types and loom concepts in many geographically distant cultures that is of greater relevance. A brief global survey between about 400 BC and AD 600 reveals thriving textile production, with each region employing a range of techniques, materials and looms. Among the cultures of the Peruvian and Bolivian highlands and coastal Peru and northern Chile, all processes were fully developed by about 400 BC. In the south-coast Paracas culture,

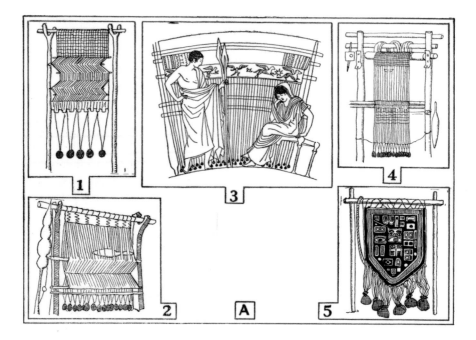

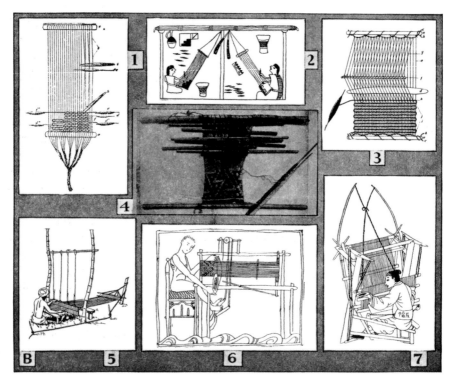

stem-stitch embroidery was particularly prevalent, but on the loom they also used looped, leno, gauze and compound weaves, all of which are also found in Chinese and central Asian textiles. On the other hand, the succeeding and more southerly Peruvian Nazca culture (200 BC to AD 600) favoured brightly coloured wool-faced tapestry, allowing a comparison with Coptic Egypt: both cultures also used sprang, cross-looped knitting and garment shaping on the loom. Painted and wax-resisted textiles were made in the Paracas and Nazca periods (900 BC to AD 600), and these and the complex tie-and-dye and pile-woven cloths of the coastal Tiahuanaco culture (AD 500–700) parallel finds scattered across Eurasia. Aspects of Andean looms – particularly the use of shed swords for pattering – can also be found in Scandinavia, China and (as a result of southwards migrations from the latter) Thailand, where this technique survives today, as it does in Peru.

Techniques obviously can evolve without input from elsewhere. Where textiles *are* imported, two things are certain: they are not initially available locally, and they are replaced whenever possible by indigenous varieties replicating the technique and/or design. Designs quickly transfer if the imagery becomes an important indication of loyalty, status or new ideological systems, often themselves introduced by the importers. Within South America such transmissions along the Andes and into the Pacific coastal regions are significant in the absence of written histories, and have allowed the identification of numerous distinct cultures and their points of contact. These are most evident in the transmission of imagery, though they are also apparent in, for example, the spread of interlocking tapestry techniques from the wool-rich highlands to the Nazca (where plant fibres were more common and so often only the weft was of wool). Further to the north, a different tapestry technique – leaving a slit between adjacent colours – is one feature that distinguishes the coastal Moche (AD 100–800) as an independent culture.

Many developments in this period result from an urge to make textiles iconographical, that is, displaying abstract or pictorial motifs meaningful within a particular culture. It is on this basis alone that the silks of Sasanian Persia have been identified. The second of two native nomad tribes to control the lands from western Iraq to central Asia, the Sasanians (AD 224–642) inherited a tradition of weaving Chinese silk threads and during the 3rd century AD developed sericulture in their Caspian satrapies (provinces), from where silk was exported to the Byzantine

60. There have been many types of warp-weighted (A) and two-beam (B) tensioned looms. In use between 750 BC and AD 600 were A1–4 (a descendant of the Neolithic Swiss type and examples from Scandinavia, 5th-century BC Greece and Iceland; A5 is later and Haida Alaskan). The tensioned looms B1–4 are Peruvian, with B2 showing the backstrap loom in use. The remainder are a horizontal ground loom, a treadle loom of the type known in the eastern Mediterranean and Egypt prior to AD 500 (and used in Europe by a century or so later) and a Chinese weaver-tensioned treadle loom. All are still used today in one form or other.

61

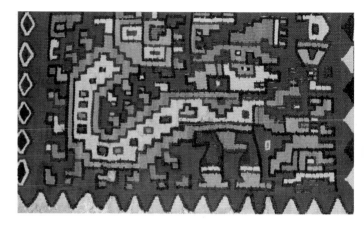

61. A Moche camelid tunic border of AD 100–800 is woven in slit tapestry, a technique that makes no interlock between different coloured wefts and that can accommodate far finer details than typically found in warp-interlock tapestry. Collection David Bernstein, New York.

62. The sophistication of Peruvian cloth structures can be appreciated in this AD 200–600 Nazca camelid 'scaffold' weave (also called warp-interlock tapestry). It is plain-woven and does not use the weft-faced tapestry construction at all. Instead, the usually continuous warp is interlocked with another of a different colour, as where the blacks and golds exchange. Collection David Bernstein, New York.

empire and central Asia. They established weaving in Susiana (now Khuzistan, Iran) and controlled Syria from AD 241 to 272, through which it is presumed they too acquired the drawloom. They gathered great wealth from their position on the Silk Route, extracting tolls and threatening Roman and Byzantine supplies to such a degree that between AD 240 and 440 the Egyptians sent ships to China by way of India and modern-day Sri Lanka. After regaining Syria, the Byzantines established sericulture there by about AD 400. Egypt imported silks from both Persia and Syria, and some of those found at Antinoë (AD 250–500) constitute the first evidence of the use of a drawloom. However, it is not until much later that Egyptian finds can be related firmly to surviving Sasanian imagery (see Chapter 4).

This highlights the issue of the origin of things and the pertinence of Pliny's history. He wrote of the world as he knew it,

63. Widely made in the 5th century AD, small Egyptian tapestry panels such as this were worked in wool onto linen warps as the weaving of plain linen cloth progressed. Many survive cut away from the linen surround.

64

64. Found in Antinoë, Egypt, but probably Sasanian Persian, this silk of AD 250–500 has imagery that derives from different coloured wefts almost entirely covering the warps; often called *samitum*, it is the first loom-woven construction to rival the pictorial capacity of tapestry. Its complex structure suggests the use of a drawloom.

65. Judging from the number interred with European rulers and saints, the most prestigious textiles of the early Middle Ages (AD 600–800) were silk *samitum* made in Sasanian Persia – the Iranian and Iraqi parts of which were Muslim after 651 – or imitated in imperial workshops in Constantinople. This example, from the treasury of St Ursula, Cologne, depicts a royal hunter dressed in Sasanian style.

as do writers today. Yet knowledge of this period is changing rapidly as a result of both new archaeological techniques and research carried out in more recent times. Against a background of the thousands of excavations completed since 1970 and older finds still awaiting analysis, there are many elaborations and challenges to come. Recent excavations at western Iraq's Tar Caves, for example, found thousands of cloths dating from 125 BC to AD 500. These demonstrate both the *status quo* and change: lots of wool and some linen, but now also resist-dyed cotton; twills, embroidered fabrics and wool-faced tapestry, some like those made in Egypt, but also pile fragments, all but the latter probably on their way eastwards. So far, however, no Sasanian silks have been discovered close to their place of origin. The vexing questions of who invented what remain. The very problem of attribution is important in its own right as evidence of textile trade and the social and literal currency of cloth. As textiles moved across time and space, they not only transmitted commercially valuable technical knowledge, but their very ownership constituted great riches in the form of loyalties, power or prestige.

63

Chapter 4:   Church and State AD 600–1500

From the rise of Islam to the European awareness of the Americas, this is a period of extensive ideological and cultural change. In AD 600 China had been riven by four centuries of internal strife, reunited only under the Tang Dynasty (618–906). Much of the Mediterranean and Middle East was in disarray, the latter changing in ethnic composition as Turkic tribes moved southwards from northeastern Siberia. Originating in Arabia, Islam spread rapidly through conquest after the death of its founder, the prophet and merchant Muhammad, in 632. By 651 Islamic caliphs ruled Syria, Palestine, Sasanian Iraq, Egypt and finally Sasanian Iran. Composed of decentralized states aligned (after 661) to Shi'i or Sunni sects, some hundred years later Sunni Islam extended into the borders of China, deep into the northern African coast and across southern Iberia. Of these conquests, Syria and Egypt had been wrested from the Byzantine empire, which remained ideologically linked to the western Christian states until 1054, when a liturgical dispute led to the division between the Byzantine (Orthodox) and Roman (Catholic) churches. This schism marked the end of the early Middle Ages in Europe and the emergence of an increasingly powerful 'Latin' alliance in western Europe. It also coincided with the Turkic Seljuk conquest of Anatolia, which further threatened the Byzantine empire.

Textiles in this period were in many respects conservative. The Egyptians continued to weave linens and tapestry, and everywhere creativity was limited mainly to subtle improvements in technology or variations in cloth structure as seen in Chinese Song damasks (960–1279), which include the first extant example of a satin weave. The Silk Route was disrupted (but restored) by the rise of the Mongols in the early 13th century and their conquests in China, where they eventually established the Yuan Dynasty (1279–1368). By the 1450s Mongolian rulers held almost all the territory bounded by Korea, Vietnam, Syria and Poland. Entire cities were destroyed during the devastation wreaked by the Mongol Timur (or Tamerlane, c. 1336–1405) as he swept from Samarkand across Russia, Mongolia, Persia, Anatolia and India. Artisans were spared, treated as booty and relocated, and these enforced migrations hastened the dispersal of techniques. Weavers from Herat (in

66. Said to have been found in the tomb of the Ming Dynasty emperor Hsiian-tê (Xuande), this fragment of silk and gilt thread *kesi* (tapestry) of 1426–35 depicts a frontal dragon above a flaming pearl. The surrounding cloud motifs were already long established within Chinese iconography and epitomize the conservatism of this period. The use of such cosmological emblems spread (see ill. 111) and continued into the 20th century.

67. Incorporating a weft of flat gilt membrane on a satin ground, this silk epitomizes Mongolian rulers' taste for gold thread-laden cloths, or *nāsij*. It was made in Turkestan or China between about 1280 and 1370, most probably by Muslim weavers.

68. Although this 8th-century eastern Mediterranean silk *samitum* depicts the Annunciation, with a few alterations its enthroned figure could represent 'State' rather than 'Church'. Closely entwined in this period, both were essentially conservative; one result was the longevity throughout Eurasia of the roundel arrangement and floral motifs seen here.

Afghanistan), who were known for their gold-woven silks and silver brocading, were removed to the Chinese Uighur region in 1222 and returned fifteen years later when their city was rebuilt. By 1260, Chinese craftsmen were at work in Tabriz, also famed for its golden cloths or *nāsij*. The Mongolian preference for these – as tributes, taxes or in trade – ensured the maintenance of conquered cities' imperial workshops (such as those in Baghdad) and the introduction of such techniques as far west as Armenia. Figured velvet weaving now appears in Yuan China and, by 1350, in India. In about 1400 *kesi* was introduced from China to Japan, where it was called *tsuzure-ori*, or 'fingernail weave'. Such diffusion is typical of this era of 'Church' and 'State'.

During the 11th and 12th centuries sericulture and silk weaving were established by Middle Eastern peoples in southern Italy and Sicily, where under Frederick II (1194–1250) dyeing was a Jewish monopoly, just as were silk processing and weaving. To mitigate the rising strength of Islamic states, the Pope formed an alliance with the Chinese Mongols, the Pax Mongolica (1260–1368), and this contributed greatly to the development of brocaded silk and velvet weaving in Italy. The Angevin conquest of Sicily in 1266 consolidated the position of Lucca, with the largest Jewish population north of Rome, as the first important Italian silk-weaving centre. Nevertheless, Byzantine weavers provided the West's most sumptuous silks, even after the fall of Constantinople to the Latins in 1204. Together with Persian and Middle Eastern Islamic weavers and embroiderers – many in formerly Byzantine Syrian workshops – they supplied and inspired the silken splendour characteristic of courts and ceremonies throughout Eurasia until the Byzantine empire itself was overrun by the Ottomans in 1453.

69. Probably made for King Roger (1130–54) and used by later German kings and Habsburg emperors, this red silk twill coronation mantle was embroidered in 1133–34 in Palermo, Sicily, facts recorded in the *tiraz*-like Kufic inscription. Worked in coloured silks, couched gold threads, and ornaments, pearls, enamels and jewels, the lion and camel represent Christianity triumphant over Islam.

70. Undoubtedly dispersed by Muslim artisans, decorative quilting was one of the 'cotton techniques' adopted throughout Europe by the 14th century (although protective linen doublets wadded with raw wool or cotton were made much earlier). This quilt, which depicts the Tristram legend in back-stitched trapunto and running stitches, was worked in 1392 for Sicilian aristocrats.

To the west, life was even more uncertain. The 'barbarian' Franks from the Rhineland had captured Gaul during the 5th and 6th centuries, but had neither Roman law, with its strong administration, nor great cities as centres of trade and sources of labour. Roman Britons had been overrun by various tribes from modern-day Germany, Denmark and the Netherlands, and from 601 were focused on converting these invaders to Christianity. Expanses of Italy came first under the control of Byzantine governors (584–751) and then the new so-called 'Latin' world, an amalgam of Frankish and Italian Christian cultures solidified by Charlemagne (742–814), who also added large areas of Germany to his domain. Crowned emperor by Pope Leo III in 800, Charlemagne established the pattern of Christian courts, complete with lavish silks and embroideries, that defined ever larger areas of Europe. Between around 772 and his death, Charlemagne's extensive conquests included the pagan Saxons of the Elbe valley, who were forced to convert to Christianity and were scattered over his lands. At his death, power passed into the hands of large landholders who exercised power in their own regions, much like the caliphs of Islam. At the same time arose the Nordic Viking sea warriors, whose vibrant textile culture –

including complex tablet-woven braids and hangings in wrapped and woven tapestry – spread with them to settlements in the northern British Isles, Normandy, Greenland, Vinland (probably Newfoundland) and the eastern Baltic. From here exchange for silks and other luxuries took Viking textiles all the way to Constantinople and the mouth of the Volga river.

The treadle loom, documented in Syria and Egypt prior to the 6th century, reached Europe in the early Middle Ages. With the decline of the Vikings and the relative calm of the ensuing High Middle Ages (1050–1300) it began to displace the warp-weighted loom, except in northern Scandinavia and Iceland. Three times more productive than the loom it replaced, it was an essential part of the revival of trade and the emergence of prosperous cities with a middle class. However, disruptive forces were never far away. The seven crusades between 1095 and 1291 led to cross-cultural encounters that disseminated ideas and stimulated East–West trade, but also ensured continued upheaval. In Iberia and southern Italy, friendly and hostile exchanges alike aided the introduction of Muslim textile techniques, some of which quite possibly had origins in India. Chief among these were cotton carding, wheel spinning of weft yarns and pattern knitting (known in Arabia and India from the 9th century), which were introduced in the 11th, 12th and 13th centuries respectively. These newly found skills were then gradually transferred to woollen manufacture across Europe, resulting in many new variations on existing cloth 'themes'. This prosperous interlude was brought to an end by the widespread famine of the early 14th century, followed by the Black Death plague epidemic (1347–50), which swept through Egypt and Europe from Syria, killing some thirty per cent of these populations.

Such destructive events had profound consequences for textiles, causing an acute shortage of skilled workers and destroying knowledge as well as people. Particularly vulnerable to backlash from these and other calamities were the Jews, who had been highly regarded for their textile skills (especially in dyeing) since the days of the Roman Empire. Thus, labour shortages at the beginning and the end of the period covered by this chapter, and the resumption of extensive trade in the middle, accelerated the tendency towards less time-consuming textile techniques. Fulling mills were in use in Italy in the 10th century and spread northwards, marking a critical step towards industrialization with the subsequent gradual incorporation of waterpower, which was fairly widespread by 1500. Across Europe

71, 72. This silk pattern-knitted glove (seen from both sides) belonged to the Archbishop of Toledo, Rodrigo Ximénez de Rada, who died in 1247. Like other contemporary Spanish examples of fine multi-needle silk knitting, its quality indicates a well-established skill.

73. Embroidery flourished between 600 and 1500, being the most expedient method of creating detailed imagery (particularly for items whose motifs did not repeat). This Chinese or Tibetan silk damask of 1375–1475 is embellished with needle-loop and flat stitches in gilded paper and silk threads.

there emerged an increased division of labour, a trend that became associated with the introduction of the treadle loom, woollen weft preparation and, in the 13th century, the adoption of broad looms, which could make woollen cloth up to 2.5 metres (8 feet) wide. From the 13th century onwards, elaborate in-working of designs was increasingly aided by loom mechanisms or by pattern knitting. The latter required two or more needles and, for plain knitting, was also much faster than cross-loop knitting, which it replaced in Egypt. (Plain multi-needle knitting had been worked in Syria from at least the 3rd century.) Tapestry decorations, rather than being worked simultaneously with a plain cloth surround, were more typically applied as separate decorative bands or blazons. The tapestry technique itself was often replaced by embroidery which, as a quicker alternative to loom-patterned silks, provided some of the most resplendent textiles of this age. The exceptions were knotted carpets (see Chapter 6) and textiles produced in *tiraz* and similar state workshops (see p. 84). Textiles made within tribal and peasant communities everywhere appear to demonstrate similar economies but were relatively untouched by the process of proto-industrialization and thus continued to elaborate upon established techniques, particularly embroidery.

74. Religious buildings around the world often contained large iconographic panels; many were painted or stamped textiles such as this Chimu *manta* of 800–1200, with its centuries-old Peruvian symbols on a palm-leaf fibre cloth. Collection David Bernstein, New York.

75. Housed in the Shosoin temple treasury, Japan, this Tang Chinese silk of 620–700 imitates a Sasanian *samitum*. The details of the winged creature and roundel became more fluid in the translation, but the weave structure was copied precisely.

In either case, this is the first period thoroughly covered by illustrated volumes and academic essays detailing textile structures, techniques and designs, and examining, over ever wider regions, the development and use of textiles and their points of inter-cultural exchange. Aside from Andean textiles, those surviving from the Americas now include substantial numbers from the Prehistoric Southwest and, between about 1250 and 1519, some examples from Precolumbian Mesoamerica. Sub-Saharan textiles enter the picture in the 9th century. Many of these were painted or pattern dyed and are discussed in Chapter 7 together with those of other cultures such as the Japanese (whose extant textile tradition begins with an embroidery of about 622). Despite individual differences, there seems to be a worldwide need – in autocratic feudal confederacies and tribal societies alike – to emphasize cultural certainties, expressed most commonly through textiles and associated regulations.

The most visible evidence of the importance of the *status quo* was the longevity of certain designs. Among these were Sasanian Persian patterns with a symmetrical arrangement of figures or animals, often confronted, set within a roundel itself filled with decorative devices. The adoption of local conventions by Islamic authorities preserved existing state workshops and the Sasanian patterns (which were also made in Constantinople) produced in them. This style rapidly dispersed even further, by

76. In this Byzantine silk *samitum* from an Italian reliquary of about 750, the arrangement echoes Sasanian patterns, as do some individual motifs, such as the 'tree of life' and the tunics worn by the hunters. Such arrangement of motifs had a long life, and similar roundels can still be found in textiles produced in the 1800s (see ills 100–102). Their scale, typically about 25 centimetres (10 inches) in diameter, was also maintained.

way of Persia and Islamic Soghdia (western Turkestan) – where silks also bore hunting scenes, confronted animals and Sasanian-style 'tree of life' designs and roundels – to Tang China (618–906). Relationships between the Japanese and Tang cultures, via Korea (where sericulture had been introduced in around 200), can account for similar designs in Japan. Hundreds of examples across Eurasia attest to their popularity. Many that survive in Christian churches were, in the first instance, 'payment' for military support provided to the Byzantines by Italians, Bulgars, Russians and Austro-Germans. (The latter succeeded in 962 to Charlemagne's dynasty and as Holy Roman Emperors vied with the Papacy for control of Europe.) In Spain, where sericulture had been introduced by the Moors in 712, the caliphate capital of Cordoba was established by the Sunni survivors of the first Syrian Umayyad dynasty (755–1031), bringing *tiraz* workshops to it and other Andalusian cities. In the 9th century, weavers from Baghdad – which between 750 and 940 was the seat of the Abbasid Caliphate of Syria and Egypt – set up additional workshops in Spain that for another three hundred or so years produced designs based on Sasanian/Byzantine prototypes. These were made on drawlooms, as they were elsewhere.

The drawloom circumvented the need for numerous hand-inserted patterning rods or foot treadles by inserting each warp

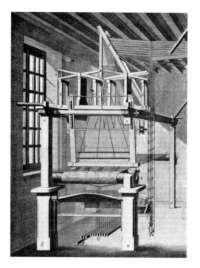

through a rising cord (leash) which, when drawn up, lifted that warp. The leashes were raised according to the desired pattern by assistants often known as draw-boys or draw-girls. The superstructure supporting the cords (which might be pulled from a platform at the top or by way of pulleys from the side) could be added to any type of horizontal loom, weaver-tensioned, warp-weighted or framed. The ground weave (for much of this period typically a weft-faced twill) continued to be controlled by harnesses whose actions were overridden by the leashes. Although still labour intensive, leashes controlling comparable points in any symmetrical pattern could be raised simultaneously by tying them together. The result was that by pulling a sequence for one motif it appeared from selvedge to selvedge half as many times as the number of leashes in each bundle. This had two consequences. Small patterns were especially time-saving and so those based on 'powderings' of motifs and lozenge-like structures became common. Once the leashes were bunched and harnesses threaded it was economical to keep these arrangements, so looms soon became dedicated to particular ground weaves and repeat sizes, a feature contributing to the longevity of structural and design elements. Until the 1400s, patterns seldom exceeded 75 centimetres (30 inches) in height.

Especially prevalent among roundel designs were those with charioteer and hunting themes, represented by horseriders, lions, eagles, elephants and bulls. These continued to be woven in Byzantine workshops even after the two periods of iconoclasm (726–87 and 815–43) banned narrative Christian themes.

Hunting themes had an obvious appeal to feudal lords, who were essentially military leaders. Indeed, powerful and swift beasts, especially lions and leopards, were frequently adopted as royal and civic insignia in feudal societies around the world; Peruvian textiles throughout this period exhibit but one of many expressions of the awe of the hunter-cat. It is telling of the intimate connections between Church and State that the same beasts and birds frequently occurred as symbols of the spiritual realm. In the Orthodox church of the 10th to 12th centuries, for example, the eagle and griffin represented heavenly flight. Similar concepts are widely recorded. Winged creatures and confronted motifs, particularly birds, were already meaningful symbols, the former long familiar within Persia and dominant among both Tiahuanaco and Huari Peruvian textile imagery of 500–700, the latter already established in Chinese iconography. During the mid-6th and early 7th centuries, the Japanese had embraced Buddhism and Chinese cosmology respectively and the resulting emblems – called *yūsoku* in Japan – now became standardized around twenty-seven basic groups. In a still largely illiterate world, many of these anthropomorphized motifs tapped so deeply into the universal desire to understand existence that they became fossilized and for centuries thereafter remained potent emblems of particular world views. For example, as the Iranian mystical sect of Islamic Sufi

78. Perhaps the most ubiquitous Eurasian motifs between 600 and 1500 were the griffin and the large-winged bird, both of which appear in this 12th-century Syrian silk found in an Egyptian grave.

79. Illustrating both the type of geometric patterns preferred by Sunni Muslims and *tiraz* production (see p. 84), this silk fabric was woven with Arabic inscriptions in a Nasrid caliphate workshop in 15th-century Spain.

coalesced in the 8th and 9th centuries, it adopted the confronted or two-headed bird – often the peacock – as a symbol of its reciprocal mirrored view of the universe.

The use of such emblems among Muslims highlights the deepest theoretical divide between the Shi'i, who allowed representations of nature, and the Sunni, who did not. In practice, however, the division was never rigid. Persian caliphs were often Sunni in persuasion, but nevertheless maintained local textile designs, even if in simplified form. The entirely abstract, complex geometric patterns approved by the Sunni are best represented by those found in Iberia under the Nasrid caliphs (1230–1492). Even here, however, the influence already noted of the Moors and Baghdad weavers was followed by influences from Cairo, the seat of the Shi'i Fatimid dynasty, who held the allegiance of Egypt and Syria from 969 to 1171. The rise of the Sunni Seljuk Turks in 11th- and 12th-century Persia and Anatolia increased both the abstraction and elaboration of patterns, but throughout the entire period even the most decorative Islamic textiles had no overtly religious motifs, a feature that readily facilitated their use and imitation in other cultures. Thus, two-headed birds, particularly eagles, became emblematic of Christian Orthodox and Roman Catholic sovereignties.

This was true even of *tiraz*, literally meaning embroidery but also denoting any Islamic textile carrying an embroidered or inlaid tapestry-woven inscription and, more generally, the caliphate workshops, whether *khassa* (exclusive to the court) or *amma* (available for purchase). These workshops produced the finest embroidered and woven silks and, like the Sasanian and Byzantine royal workshops before them, were state controlled and carefully guarded due to the bullion embroidery produced within. The earliest known *khassa* dates from 724 to 743, though they are thought to have emerged in the late 7th century. Inscribed textiles were particularly associated with Fatimid Egypt, where the Copts had previously interwoven Greek inscriptions. The thousands of surviving *tiraz* demonstrate a change in the mid-11th century to shorter inscriptions or entirely decorative ones thus suitable only for non-Islamic or illiterate Islamic populations. The use of *tiraz* was only widespread throughout Islam until 1293, when the Mongols banned them except for court use. Thereafter they are well documented in Yuan China, and Mongolian conquests to the west coincided with the introduction of script borders in Orthodox embroidery in the early 15th century. Here and elsewhere *tiraz* influence

lingered, and inscribed textiles were still sold in Cairo even after the closure of the Egyptian caliphate workshops in about 1341.

Islamic *tiraz* functioned as a 'contract' between the caliph and his people. Distributed as a sign of patronage and accepted as acknowledgment of his authority, they were also purchased and given to the caliph in lieu of taxes and as tribute. The long-established and more general tribute system also remained in place and the many gifts from wealthy donors to temples, churches and monasteries were an extension of this practice. As a means of embodying the mutual obligations within a society, it has many parallels elsewhere. Mesoamerican pictographic codices include notations of the Aztec empire's tribute tallies illustrating both the designs and quantities of *mantas* or mantles – in the thousands – that were expected to arrive from the provinces every eighty days. Their Precolumbian contemporaries, the Andean Inkas (1438–1532), preserved from their preceding cultures a very similar system. Expressed as 'offerings', they constituted a well-defined exchange between the right to farm 'Crown' or 'Church' lands and use communal supplies of wool and cotton, and the obligation to work the land and weave cloth for the authorities in return.

Such pacts also summarize the position of Old World serfs. For those tied to monastic lands, this 'gift' of an often large proportion of their output in exchange for protection, subsistence and prayer survives in the less burdensome present-day meaning of tithing. Not surprisingly, the emerging independent weaver-drapers in Europe (*drapiers, lanaiuoli,* or clothiers) structured their businesses along the same lines. The materials belonged to the clothier and were distributed among workers

80. Known as the Shroud of St Josse, and kept for many centuries in a Parisian church, this Shi'i *tiraz* of about 950 contains recognizable camels and elephants. Such motifs are appropriate to its origins in Khorasan, situated in the ancient West Caspian corridor between the steppes and northern Iran, through which a near-constant stream of invaders and traders travelled.

81. Within Latin American cultures cotton was a prestigious fibre; here it has been tapestry-woven into a Pachacamac sample of 1000–1350. The sample retains its own small loom (not illustrated), which reflects the Peruvian custom of burying weavers with tools of their trade. Collection David Bernstein, New York.

82. In Madagascar, the highland Merina preserve ties to southeast Asia through both their language and their weaving practice. Since 1500 they have woven narrow silk cloths using traditional motifs and techniques for special events from sacred offerings to diplomatic presents. The patterns, picked out by hand from individual leashes, come from Indonesia. The Malagasy terms for writing and preparing the loom are interchangable.

who were obliged to return rovings, slivers, spun yarns or prepared warps – all made with their own tools – in exchange for the right to that work and payment in cash or in kind. Weaving was typically done on looms owned by the clothier but was otherwise also piecework. This concept became known as 'putting-out' and still exists today. In the absence of contractual laws, allegiances such as these extended from the clothiers to their customers, the merchants and finishers. The latter under-took fulling, tentering (stretching back into shape) and shearing, all important stages in woollen and some serge production, while others specialized in different categories of piece dyeing, including the over-dyeing of woad fibre-dyed wools or the carefully guarded process of scarlet dyeing. Merchant-drapers were clothiers who also finished and dyed cloths and many became wealthy in the process, thus entering the brotherhood of the urban elite.

In hierarchical societies the significance of textiles was more than a matter of the best to the richest (although that was also true). While it is easy to understand the awe inspired by the sumptuous woven, embroidered and jewel- or metal thread-encrusted silks exclusive to nobility in this period, rank and fealty were also denoted in many other ways. The Sufi were literally 'wearers of woollen cloth', eschewing the silks of the court, as did many monastics elsewhere. The earliest Burmans of Myanmar, the Pyu (500–900), were described by Tang chroniclers as weavers of fine cotton cloth, used in preference to silk because, as devout Buddhists (a religion otherwise closely associated with silk), they refused to kill the silkworms. Similar restrictions applied to some followers of Hinduism, an ancient amalgam of religious beliefs and institutions that had evolved in India. As Buddhism, Hinduism and Islam were dispersed, so too was knowledge of cotton preparation and cultivation. One result of this was the introduction of cotton crops in the 8th century to the Tarim Basin.

Among Prehistoric Southwestern tribes, cotton (whose cultivation had been introduced from Mexico to the southern Arizonan Hohokam by 500 and passed by them to the Mogollon and Anasazi after about 1100) had several ritual and spiritual meanings, including symbolizing clouds. In the bast-based Mesoamerican textile culture, cotton was *the* luxury fibre, enhanced by embroidery using silken yarns of rabbit underbelly fur or, occasionally, wild silk, plumage, shells, stones and precious metals. Although for the Inkas the most valued object was weft-faced tapestry, in Peru as late as the 18th century one cotton cloth *manta* (blanket) given in tribute was worth two made of wool. (The tribute system continued to be used, and sometimes abused, by Spanish colonialists throughout the Americas.)

That few cotton cloths survive in Eurasia from this period may be due not to their lack of use or regard, but rather to the introduction of rag-paper-making from the East in the 8th century (although there it was made of hempen rags and mulberry bark). Nevertheless, in Europe at this time cotton appears to have been mainly used for candlewicks, while luxury cloths were

instead being made of the finest wool fibres obtained from central England. A 30-metre (32-yard) piece of such broadcloth took about thirty people one month to make. Of these, only two would have been weavers. Yarn preparation accounted for close to half of the unfinished cloth's cost and ensured supple draping qualities, with the most sought-after being those dyed scarlet.

Colours alone could denote rank. A 10th-century Byzantine code reiterated the ban on purple dyes for private manufacture. Islamic and Eastern rulers similarly took particular colours as symbols of their dynasties. In 9th-century Islam, non-Muslims were required to wear a honey colour, and as a result the Byzantines were known in Arabic as the 'safflower people'. Yellow for 'outsiders' was long maintained in the West, and this meaning may also have been intended when it was adopted by the warrior Mamluk sultans (who ruled Egypt, Syria and much of Libya and the Sudan between 1250 and 1517). Elsewhere the colour yellow was used to signify 'insiders'. For example, in hier-archical Oceanic societies it was reserved, together with red, for the *tiputas* of chieftains and others of high status. The Japanese had a complex system of rank colours that only gradually declined under the shoguns (from 1192), who adopted aspects of commoners' dress and, as in the West, developed armour initially based entirely on textile techniques. This was the age of pennants, heraldry and magnificent tents and horse trappings, all of which used colour as their primary distinguishing feature, underscoring the way it so readily identifies 'us' from 'them'. Only at close quarters were motifs important; a Byzantine silk woven with the monogram of the Emperor Heraclius (610–641) is an early surviving example of this practice, which could also be achieved by stamping, painting and embroidery. In Islam the wearing of amiral blazons ('rank badges' in the Far East) was associated with the Mamluks.

Much that is known about textile attributes comes from sumptuary laws. These attempts to prevent excess of finery pro-hibited or regulated the use of many elements of dress: colours, fibres, designs, metal embroidery and furs. In Byzantine, Islamic and Eastern cultures these seem principally to apply to men. However, such legislation was difficult to enforce because of the constant circulation of second-hand textiles, including some of the finest quality. Those made for the 1327 coronation of the English king Edward III were afterwards given away as gratu-ities and alms, the poor receiving most of the fifteen pieces of 'candlewickstreet' carpet, a term evoking the looped or tufted

84. Prized 'tartar cloths' containing wefts of flat gilt membrane were highly influential on southern European weavers. Their patterns had even wider impact, and the contrapuntal arrangement seen in this late 13th- or 14th-century Sino-Mongolian design remained fashionable in Europe for another 300 years.

cottons known later. Hundreds of cloth names and technical nuances can be gleaned from the many royal accounts, statutes and guild regulations of this period but, as is the case here, it is often not possible to associate terms with surviving textiles. The attribution of surviving examples is only further complicated by the Norman conquest of Sicily and their establishment in 1147 of workshops in Palermo using native Islamic embroiderers and Byzantine weavers captured in the Peloponnese. This began the expansion of silk weaving into southern Italy (also under Norman control by this time). There and elsewhere in the Mediterranean many new textile centres emerged during the 12th and 13th centuries as the Islamic and Byzantine empires weakened. And the simultaneous influence of 'tartar' cloths available as a result of the Pax Mongolica introduced Sino-Mongolian designs and techniques to Europe, especially gold brocading. By 1500 several Italian city-states had become significant centres for silk production (see Chapter 5).

Faced with the incursion of new textiles and processes, many of those involved in textile manufacture at this time sought security and order, and this anxiety is reflected in many contemporary documents. Guild regulations and statutes everywhere demonstrate the desire to prevent adulteration of materials or techniques – particularly important for those catering for export markets – and reveal the attempts made by trades to both attain and maintain status. This is particularly the case in Europe, where weaver-drapers fought to gain supremacy over dyers and finishers, and manufacturing centres vied for supremacy. After around 1240 strife was widespread, with both economic gain and political power at stake. In this increasingly secular and market-driven world, the production and role of textiles began to change. While still esteemed as insights into the eternal world – and, for the finest cloths, as assurances in life – Western textiles were moving inexorably towards industrialization and the separation from art that this implies.

Chapter 5: Western Ideas and Styles Dispersed 1300–1900

The West in this period includes Muscovite and Romanov Russia and, increasingly from 1500, areas of North America. Despite gradual urbanization and the rise of other specialist crafts, the principal luxuries remained embroidery, tapestry and woven or knitted silks and wools. Together with carpets (see Chapter 6) they set the dominant tone for interiors until the early 20th-century movements towards simplicity, as well as fuelling the increasingly rapid changes in clothing fashions. Particularly important in these respects were embroidery and similarly decorative additions, such as the tassels, cords, edgings, braids and ribbons that became known as 'passementerie' if twisted or plaited, and included many 'small wares', both band- and loom-woven. All of these might be sold by 'lace-men' (as, from 1600 or so, was lace as it would be recognized today – see Chapter 8), and were frequently the most expensive and expressive elements of dress and furnishings in peasant and urban cultures alike. Other occasions of public display throughout this period – whether coronations, feast days, civic processions, military splendour or the carriages and livery of the elite – also depended on these same textiles. The development of embroidery, tapestry and weaving is closely aligned to innovations in other disciplines such as painting, wood carving, engraving or lithography. Only in the 18th century did printed cottons – and wallpapers – become more widespread, and another century passed before prints threatened the supremacy of the established textile forms. The significance of traditional techniques, so clearly expressive of the fact that they are handmade, is underlined by the fact that their stylistic evolution is extremely well charted. Here, however, the emphasis is placed on the skills required in their making and the people who made them.

A complex set of tastes and influences acted upon artisans of this period. Of importance at the outset were a number of regions with connections to Constantinople and the Levant with their rich textile traditions. In northern Europe this influence was felt in tapestry and embroidery, the latter providing an alternative to costly and scarce imported figured silks. In 1204 the Flemish king Baldwin IX had conquered Constantinople, thus creating close links between that city and Flanders (which

85. The differentiation between dress and furnishing textiles in the West only emerged in the 1730s; even then the most fashionable attire was identified by details such as this silk and gilt thread embroidered stomacher and collar, thought to be Italian.

86. Woven at the Royal Beauvais Tapestry Manufactory using cartoons produced by Jean-Baptiste Monnoyer in the 1680s, this tapestry belongs to a set of about six today known as the 'Grotesques de Bérain'. Designed to be enlarged or reduced according to their final location, at least 40 sets were sold, 13 by 1694 and the last in 1732.

87. In the upper Rhineland during the late Middle Ages many tapestry workshops were kept active producing hangings for pageants and processions, or as tributes. This late 15th-century panel, only 74 centimetres (29 inches) high, is a typical production, and one of only 51 surviving 15th-century Strasbourg tapestries.

covered northern France, most of present-day Belgium and part of the Netherlands). As a result, Flanders became a major centre of northern textile commerce. Not far away, some fifty years later, the first recorded Parisian tapestry weavers made what was called *tapis sarazinois* ('Sarasen' tapestry), a legacy of their Middle Eastern source of the French 'high warp' or upright tapestry loom. (Tapestry made on a horizontal loom was called 'low warp', and this technique was already in evidence throughout northern and central Europe by this time.)

In contrast, Near Eastern influence on silk and metal thread producers and weavers was most evident in Italy. Foremost among the weavers in 1300 were those of Lucca, although by the end of the century they had been eclipsed by those in Florence, Genoa and Venice (the latter city-state being the point of onward trade for Eastern finished goods and Italy's own silk and metal threads). Many different weaves were made in these and other Italian cities, including vast quantities of simpler silks woven on treadle looms. Florence produced fine woollens from English

88. The impact of 'tartar cloths' can be seen in this 14th-century northern Italian silk, particularly in the dynamic arrangement of birds and beasts amid an array of exotic foliage. A less obvious influence is evident in the compound weave structure, which incorporates red, black and white silk brocading.

wool, and its fulling mills finished cloths woven for Italian merchants as far afield as Flanders. In the early 14th century, Italian drawloom weavers began to use more complex cloth structures and asymmetrical designs, most probably derived from the 'tartar cloths' imported under the Pax Mongolica. Among the new cloth structures were compound weaves such as cloth of gold, and figured velvets (plain velvets were already woven in Italy). Lucca was especially known for compound weaves, although both techniques were used in rival Italian cities by the 1400s. They were also known in Spain (still partly Islamic until 1492), which traded with Genoa and had a long-established tradition of sericulture and allied trades.

The designs radiating from a growing number of northern Italian weaving centres dominated tastes well into the 17th century, when their role as pacesetter was taken over by France and then later shared by England (especially for dress silks). Thus, the weaving of velvets and gold-brocaded silks in Europe originated in the south. In their absence, the area north and east of the Alps was dominated by embroidery and tapestry, which could make much greater use of local wool and linen supplies. Naturally, in other parts of Europe local materials were allied to local skills; so, from Vienna to Poland and into Russia, where freshwater pearls were plentiful, ornamentation with them was worked by specialist embroiderers. The transmission of tastes and techniques was partly governed by the religious affiliations and shifting alliances of the European royal families. The most prominent of these was the Habsburg dynasty, who first ruled in Switzerland in 1273 but came to greater power as the Holy Roman Emperors between 1438 and 1806. Of this dynasty, Charles V (1500–58) perhaps did most to diffuse styles. He inherited and brought together Burgundy, the Netherlands, the Spanish crown (including Naples and, in theory, nearly all of the Americas), and the Austro–Germanic empire itself. The fine Flemish tapestries today in Spanish collections are but one example of his influence. His successor, Rudolph II of Bohemia,

89. This figured silk velvet of about 1710 woven in France or Italy, possibly for the Polish market, demonstrates both the increasingly homogeneous tastes among European courts and the complexity of textiles made for them. Cut and uncut pile is highlighted by surrounds with no pile, a construction called ciselé voided velvet.

drew artisans from throughout his domain, and it was Spanish expertise that appears to have inspired the large pattern-knitted panels newly required to obtain master status in the guilds of Rudolph's court city, Prague. Before long, this requirement had spread to other cities in the upper Rhineland, Alsace, Austria and, by the mid-17th century, several German states.

The styles that traversed Europe did so not only through the transport of textiles from one region to another, but also through the movement of their makers. For example, by 1250 England had established a reputation for the most meticulous and sought-after embroidery, *opus anglicanum*. Such work was in demand as far away as Italy, and by the early 1300s English embroiderers were themselves at work there and as far east as Lower Saxony. After about 1350 more expedient methods of embroidery came to dominate English work and its position as leader was usurped near the end of the century by Flemish

90. (opposite) The Pienza Cope was given to that city's cathedral in 1462 by Pope Pius II but is English work (*opus anglicanum*). Taking twenty years to embroider, from 1315 to 1335, the ground is covered with a limited number of types of stitch, including stem stitch for outlining, split stitch for modelling the faces and hands, and – thought to be its distinctive characteristic – underside couching of gold threads.

91. Attributed to the Brussels atelier of Cornelius Tons, this tapestry belongs to a set probably made for the Italian Farnese family and telling the story of Scipio. Designed in Mantua (possibly at the instigation of Charles V), the set was first woven in 1532 when commissioned by François I of France from an important Flemish merchant, Marc Crétif. Further sets were woven in the 16th and 17th centuries for Habsburg, Swedish, Austrian and French aristocrats.

artisans, many of whom were kept busy by the courts of the Dukes of Burgundy. The technique associated with this region is *or nué*, in which realistic drapery is suggested by the use of gold threads overstitched with variously shaded and spaced silk threads. This was adopted in England in the 15th century but never with the same proficiency (suggesting that it was acquired by observation rather than first-hand tutelage). *Or nué* was also introduced to workshops in Austria, France and Italy by Flemish masters. Some of the earliest of these new workshops were established by 1391 in Barcelona and elsewhere in Spain, several of which survived well into the 16th century, after which the influence of Flemish embroidery styles began to wane.

The importance of Flanders as a textile centre cannot be overemphasized. The basic prerequisite for high-quality work was wealthy patrons, and the region had plenty of these. Its capital, Bruges, was the mercantile centre for some hundred towns belonging to the powerful northern European trading fraternity, the Hanseatic League, and it was linked by sea (and increasingly canals) to other European ports. Bruges was well known for its tapestry in the 14th century, as were the Flemish towns of Tournai, Oudenarde and the established centre for wool trade and weaving, Brussels. Just to the south, in Artois, is Arras, the town credited with the most famous medieval tapestry set, the 'Angers Apocalypse' (1375–80). Tapestry ateliers located elsewhere in Europe could not match the range of expertise concentrated around this small principality. By the 15th century, Flemish ports such as Bergen-op-Zoom, Bruges and Antwerp – the latter being one of the largest seaports in the world and in the 16th century the commercial centre for all western Europe – were also important for their tapestry markets. In addition, Bruges and Antwerp were main centres for tapestry repair well into the 18th century. These were notably cosmopolitan cities: so many foreigners were to be found examining tapestries in Flemish markets that it was said to be a good 'cover' for eavesdropping on rival nations' ambassadors and envoys. The dispersal of weavers and embroiderers was undoubtedly aided by such widespread contacts, and the emergence of new workshops elsewhere was frequently dependent upon Flemish skills.

The catalogue of workshops started, run or revived by Flemish weavers gives a composite view of the nature of tapestry weaving throughout this period. Much work was done by itinerant weavers, called *tapissiers de passage*, who attended to the wants of scattered nobles – many of whom were themselves

92. Provincial designs were often a fusion of local preferences and once-fashionable urban styles. In this 1650–1700 Norwegian biblical tapestry the bustling scene and bold border owe much to textiles depicting epic Norse sagas of 500 to 800 years earlier; the less assured roundel suggests Sasanian–Byzantine models. It may have been made by one of the itinerant weavers active in Norway between the 1560s and the 1720s.

progressing through their lands during each year – and well-endowed churches. They tended to make smaller works or, it is thought, *mille fleur* designs, and while their existence has been questioned by some historians, *tapissiers de passage* were still working in Norway and Sweden until about 1725. In those countries, the practice dated back to Gustav I's retention between 1523 and 1566 of Flemish weavers and embroiderers who, having completed their service, were dispersed throughout Scandinavia. (Thereafter itinerant weavers become well documented in North America, not for pictorial tapestries, but for overshot coverlets that are similarly woollen-weft faced.) Alternatively, foreign weavers might be recruited to work on specific projects, as was the case in northern Italy. In this way in 1536 Flemish weavers joined compatriot repairers in Ferrera (where the Este tapestry workshops survived until 1582), and are credited with the formation of the ateliers in Mantua, Sienna, Florence and Rome (alongside French weavers) during the same period. In France, tapestry production at Tours had already benefited from Flemish skills when the short-lived royal workshop (*c.* 1535–47) of François I recruited weavers almost entirely from Flanders.

The majority of weavers fell into a third category. Resident in their own workshops, they were dependent upon orders from merchants or wealthy patrons, who provided the 'cartoons'. This was the case with the cartoons painted for Pope Leo X by Raphael in 1515–17 and woven in Brussels ateliers (by now the source of the finest tapestries, Arras having declined in the later 15th century). Unlike workers within the putting-out system, they financed their own materials. In these ways their working lives paralleled those of many embroiderers, knitters and fine-cloth weavers whose trades were governed by guidelines and statutes laid down by their guilds (which also operated in Islamic regions) or city corporations. These guidelines varied in detail, but agreed on general points: members should not work by candlelight or with inferior materials, nor should they work on Sundays or feast days. Apprentices (whose tenure varied from four to ten years, that for cloth weaving being the shortest) could only be engaged by those who owned a workshop and were themselves skilled, usually demonstrated by the production of a 'masterpiece'.

Such restrictions were not enforced in royal workshops, where major events such as coronations could not be predicted and where, accordingly, impromptu techniques such as gilt

93. Among the few surviving
textiles made to attain Master
status within a guild are a group
of knitted panels from central
Europe. This example, made in
Strasbourg in 1748, reflects the
lasting influence of Persian and
Ottoman designs (see Chapter 6).

stamping and painting were allowed. Embroiderers in particular were known to work through the night. This practice continued under conditions that gradually declined from the standards of the English Great Wardrobe of the 1350s (when candles and wine were provided) to the dingy workrooms providing for 'the season' some five hundred years later. The first real sign of change is the wider decline of *or nué*, although considering that a set of orphreys commissioned by the Merchants' Guild of Florence in 1466 took some twenty-three years to embroider, it is surprising that it was still another century before this technique gave way to larger (and thus faster) stitches.

By the 1520s, the Reformation was under way and northern Europe was gradually converting to Protestantism. A new category of artisan emerged: émigrés. For most of the late 16th century, religious wars raged throughout the Low Countries, France and elsewhere, and in 1576 Antwerp's tapestry market was sacked by Spanish troops. Many Protestant weavers left Flanders, finding their way to Ireland, Scotland, England, Holland, Denmark, Sweden, Switzerland and many towns in Germany. Some Catholics fled too: one colony of Flemish tapestry weavers in Castile, Spain, remained there from about 1623 to the end of the 1800s. A large number of embroiderers also left. Flemish ateliers survived, but in the 17th century their specialities became more marked, and embroiderers became known for their 'pictures', especially of flowers. The several remaining tapestry centres became distinguished on the the basis of cost, ranging from the least expensive from Oudenarde, known for its verdures (coarser variants were woven from the 16th century at Aubusson), through medium-qualities such as those made in Antwerp, to the finest and most costly from Brussels.

In 1598 French Protestants (who were known as Huguenots) were granted religious freedom and during the resulting peace a concerted effort was made to develop luxury trades. By 1607 Henry IV had established a low-warp tapestry industry with 60 looms in Paris and 20 in Amiens, run and largely staffed by Flemish weavers. In order to protect this new venture, a fifteen-year ban was placed on the importation of tapestries from Flanders. In response to such initiatives, the Flemish banned emigration but, even then, other regions continued to benefit from their skills. In England one beneficiary was the royal workshop established at Mortlake, just outside London, in 1619. The Parisian low-warp workshops were eventually amalgamated with existing high-warp ateliers into the royal manufactory,

94. Russian textile merchants and manufacturers were often indebted to western European designers and weavers. Nevertheless, by the 19th century Moscow had several entirely Russian-run textile firms including A. & W. Sapojnikoff, which exhibited this silk at the 1876 Philadelphia Centennial Exhibition. Its griffins and peacocks, set in elaborate scrolling roundels, reflect both the inherited use of roundel patterns and the then-fashionable revival of Middle Eastern styles (see Chapter 6).

the Gobelins, in 1662. In 1664 and 1665, two other centres were granted official support: Beauvais (with low-warp ateliers) and Aubusson (with its established products). Twenty years later, 86 when the protection of religious freedom was removed, many of the Aubusson weavers scattered, some providing Berlin with a workshop (1686–1714). By 1690 this upheaval had induced a revival of fortunes in the old Flemish centres, which lasted for some fifty years. Nevertheless, the Gobelins model provided inspiration for several new enterprises, all in Catholic regions. Between about 1710 and 1718, Rome, Naples, Madrid and Munich all gained subsidized ateliers; in Bavaria there were at least four other centres besides the Munich workshop (which operated until 1802). In Russia in 1716, Peter the Great established a Gobelins-style workshop in his newly founded St Petersburg, directed by the Parisian architect Le Blond and drawing weavers from both France and Flanders on five-year contracts. It survived until 1859.

Specialist textile skills were in high demand. Piece-rate payments to French weavers in 1751, for example, were between three and thirty-six times greater for compound cloths than for plain ones. While cottage spinning and weaving were widespread (and, as they became increasingly drawn into the putting-out system, very poorly paid), the elite status of specialists placed them in a different category – so much so that they were often tempted away from their home country. Certainly their trade brought with it a considerable degree of freedom. Emigration changed the nature of textiles permanently. For example, gold-brocaded silks began to be made in Paris only as a result of the improvements made to the drawloom in about 1605 by Claude Dangon, an Italian in Lyon (where elaborate silks were not made until the next century). In addition, 16th- and 17th-century migrations from both the Low Countries and France can account for the emergence of new types of worsted- 95 mix cloths and tapestry- and silk-weaving centres in England (which became so dependent on its textile trade that between 1719 and 1824 the emigration of textile specialists was forbidden by law). More émigrés arrived in Britain due to the French Revolution, this time transforming the local straw-plaiting trade. Lyon was said to have lost twenty-thousand silk weavers at this time, with such detrimental effect that in 1802 Napoleon was calling for their return. In the subsequent uprisings of 1848–51, Britain again gained French artisans, as did Patterson, New Jersey, which opened its first silk factory in 1840 and by

95. This manuscript, a catalogue of French, Dutch and English textiles, was compiled in about 1760 by Signor Mocassi to help merchants and weavers in his own country, Italy. This page shows glazed Norwich worsteds of the sort introduced to that English region more than a century before by French and Flemish émigrés.

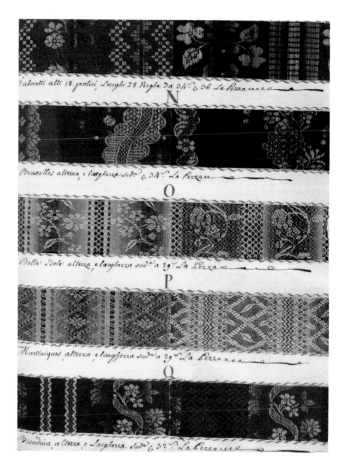

1870 had over sixty French silk dyers, weavers, finishers and merchants (although the majority were of English origins).

While artists and designers were similarly mobile, it is telling that the influential regions at any one time were those where art and technique coexisted. The northern schools of manuscript illumination were important contributors to *opus anglicanum* and Flemish textile arts, while between 1350 and 1450 the influence of Bohemian painters and embroiderers was simultaneously felt in Germany, Austria, Silesia and on the Baltic coast. Such interaction is also well charted in Italy, where in the early 1400s the Florentine painter Cennino Cennini went so far as to include instructions on textile design in his manual for painters, *Il Libro dell'Arte.* He particularly advised painters to adopt the traditional embroiderers' practice of stretching the cloth on a frame to draw the underdesign, and this canvas-stretching process was to transform painting itself, as did other textile arts. Pisanello's approach to painting in the second quarter of the 15th century, for example, drew upon Flemish tapestries and he also designed embroideries. By the time designs for orphreys 97 alone were being supplied in Florence by Botticelli (who died in 1510) there was likewise general acceptance of Cennini's comment that velvets were best embellished by such separately embroidered elements, appliquéd into place.

In some cases there were more concrete connections between those who designed and those who made luxury textiles. For example, a handful of families had ateliers in both Arras and Tournai, with a single Arras artist supplying all their cartoons. Documented examples are frequent enough to suggest that such ties were not uncommon. In Cologne, which in the 1400s was the largest northwestern German centre for embroidery and braid weaving, there were several generations of Bornheim master embroiderers, one of whom in mid-century shared a house with a leading painter, Stephan Lochner. The most famous example is that of Peter Paul Rubens (1577–1640), whose father-in-law,

96. Italian silk velvets such as the one illustrated here in detail were much sought after during the 15th and 16th centuries, often being depicted in paintings and used for vestments – in this case a chasuble of 1475–1500 made in Roman Catholic Cologne. The applied silk-embroidered linen orphrey (centre) includes a tree-like motif also typical of the town's loom-woven bands of this and the previous centuries.

97. Many medieval and Renaissance artists produced designs for textiles. This example by Pisanello or his workshop and dating to about 1449, bears the chivalric motto of Alfonso V, King of Aragon, Spain, and later also of Sicily and Naples. It was to be carried out in embroidery.

Daniel Fourment, was an Antwerp merchant specializing in finished tapestries, cartoons and materials. Fourment no doubt contributed to Rubens's enduring influence in both embroidery and tapestry. Other notable examples include the Ghent embroiderer Jakob de Rynck (c. 1680–1737), who also sold metal threads obtained in Amsterdam and Lille. (Wire drawing and the making of metal threads was done by specialists.) His eldest daughter's husband was the painter Frans Pilson (1700–84) and so it is likely that both Jakob and his son Michael, who inherited the business, obtained designs in this way. A knowledge of production techniques was especially important for those who designed for brocades and other figured loom-goods and there is ample evidence in 18th-century Lyon and other weaving centres that this often came through familial ties. Wherever possible, design and production skills, workshops and merchanting activities were passed from generation to generation, and even today there remain a few family firms that can trace their origins back to this period.

Another way in which influences were shared across media was through the guilds. These were by no means universal or identical in their make up, but do reveal that embroidery in particular was often aligned with other trades. Especially significant was the Guild of St Luke, the patron saint of painters. It is known to have absorbed Vienna's guild of embroiderers in 1446 and Westphalian (western German) pearl-workers in the following century, when it was widespread throughout central

Europe and the Low Countries. Its composition reflected individual locations, but as well as embroiderers it embraced painters, glass makers, goldsmiths, harness makers, sculptors, glaziers, potters, weavers, engravers and printers, as well as merchants of these items. Such ties may well have provided the inspiration for the sculptural or metalwork-like raised embroidery characteristic of Austria, Germany, western Poland and Hungary after about 1460, and raised work elsewhere in northern Europe during the 1600s and early 1700s. (That the Guild is today composed of physicians can be explained by the presence of dyers among its early members, as most natural dyestuffs had recognized pharmaceutical uses and were called 'drugs'.) French guilds – of which the first was established in Paris in 1272 – allowed embroiderers to choose whether to work with fabric engravers, purse makers, chasuble makers (ecclesiastical work), *tailleurs* (costume), *lingères* (linen whitework), or *tapissiers*. This last term, encompassing tapestry weavers, upholsterers and interior decorators, indicates the once-dominant role of tapestry wall- and bed-hangings in interiors. From the outset, however, such items were as often made by embroidery, appliqué, velvets, damasks and so on, and more often of wool than of silk.

99. Frequent revivals and 'borrowings' across specializations were aided from the 1500s onwards by the increasing fashion for collecting and libraries. In addition, while some technical barriers remained, by about 1735 this French brocaded silk could faithfully reproduce the landscapes, flowers and fruit often seen in earlier Flemish embroidery as a result of the development of new weave constructions that allowed more realistic shadings.

These and other design-intensive textile trades are for convenience and clarity often studied by their separate techniques, but no such clear-cut division existed. Netherlandish cushion embroiderers of the 16th to early 19th centuries followed tapestry styles, using long and short stitch. Similar parallels can be found in Scandinavia. The silk-weaving quarters of Lyon, London, Vienna and elsewhere abounded with embroiderers. In the early 1700s silk designers were inspired by laces and in the 1730s by 17th-century Flemish floral embroidery (also flourishing in Austria as a result of migration). Such exchanges were numerous and indicate which technique, whether new or newly appreciated, was the most fashionable at the time. The Gobelins also incorporated other crafts such as cabinetry and other textile specialisms such as dyeing. (The long apprenticeships of eight to ten years for tapestry weavers stemmed in part from the fact that they dyed their own wools.) In England, the royal Great

Wardrobe had moved within London to Soho and continued to produce some tapestries under Paul Saunders until about 1742. However, he was additionally a part-time cabinet maker, upholsterer and undertaker, and thus a harbinger of 'carriage trade' shops. At the same time elsewhere, tapestry weavers were already complaining about the loss of artistic independence to merchants demanding the repetitive production of cartoons. As the example of Saunders suggests, pictorial textile skills were becoming subservient to the cabinet makers and diluted in order to serve the growing number of consumers. In addition, he serves as a reminder that the role of men had increased in all aspects of professionally made textiles as a result of the development of guilds, merchanting, and the amount of capital – which men largely controlled – required to maintain high-quality production. Some specialisms, such as bullion work, even became male preserves: in Spain it was the sole embroidery done professionally by men, for bullfighters' costumes.

100. Despite the growing dominance of men in textile merchanting and management, significant numbers of women remained involved in textile making. This wall-hanging, using woollen *intarsia* (inset) appliqué with the seams and decorative accents worked in gilt membrane, was made in around 1500 in the Brigittine convent at Naantali (Finland), an influential textile centre.

Aside from the thousands undertaking put-out work of many kinds, women throughout this period dominated 'amateur' embroidery. This included the work of many expert noblewomen, of which Mary Queen of Scots (1542–87) is perhaps the best-known example. However, the pastimes and tastes of many other royal women were far more influential, in that they set the fashions for their courts, often employed their own embroiderers and, if foreign – as they frequently were – introduced styles from their homeland. Such influences often 'leapt' over great distances, as is evident in the Italianate textiles (and architecture) seen in Muscovy in the late 15th and 16th centuries. While friars were known to work embroideries (the Benedictine abbey of Admont, in Austria, is one example of note in the period 1650–1720), convent workshops were more widespread and were important sources of spun yarns, embroidery and woven cloths, as well as training. Among the most influential were the Brigittine Sisters (the Order of Our Saviour) founded in 1370 in Vadstena, Sweden, and active throughout Scandinavia and the British Isles by the next century. During the 16th and 17th centuries they founded many further convents, chiefly in Poland, France, Belgium, Spain and Mexico.

Both secular and church embroidery came to be associated with convents. The Florentine Murate in the mid-15th century reputedly produced work of a higher standard than that of the privately owned workshops in the same city. In Courtrai, Belgium, the Sion convent began embroidery in 1526 and later established their own schools. Between 1627 and about 1793, the Ursulines at Amiens were known for their embroidery, as were their sister houses in the Rhineland. They, too, were a teaching order and from their New Orleans convent spread within the United States and Canada during the 19th century. However, the most sought-after North American schools for the 'finishing' of girls in the same period were those run by the Sisters of Bethlehem (Moravian Brethren, originally from Bohemia), whose first two schools had been founded in 1749 in Bethlehem, Philadelphia. At the other end of the spectrum, both plain sewing and fine techniques were invaluable to orphans otherwise disenfranchised from the network of inherited skills and workshops, and in Paris in the 18th century many were trained at the expense of Madame de Montespan in the Convent of St Joseph.

Underlying the social trends of this entire period was the spread of knowledge and literacy, which was both welcomed and

101. By the 19th century, samplers were an important symbol of a girl's education, which was typically private or in schools run by religious organizations. This example, incorporating by-now near universal geometric and roundel motifs, was made by Ann Grimshaw in 1818, after two years at the Friends' boarding school in Ackworth, northeastern England.

ABCDEFGHIJKLMNOPQRS
TUVWXYZ. ABCDEFGHI
JKLMNOPQRSTUVWXYZ.
ABCDEFGHIJKLMNOPQRSTUVWXYZ.æœ
ABCDEFGHIJKLMNOPQRSTUVWXYZ. abcdefghi
jklmnopqrstuvwxyz. abcdefghijklmnop
rstuvwxyz. abcdefghijklmnopqrstuvwxyz. 1234567890.
1234567890. 1234567890.&c &
1234567890 Ann Grimshaw. 1818   1234567890.

resisted by the world of textiles. Guilds and state legislation often acted as conservative forces, striving to contain the dissemination of skills and designs, yet both trade and governments eventually established and supported schools for textile designers, an early example being that founded in 1683 by Flemish tapestry weavers settled in Lambeth, London. Such developments, and the rise of city corporations, diminished guild authority, and by the early 19th century they had only nominal powers. Printed patterns, first as single sheets and then, from 1524, in book form, were the product of German, Italian and

102. This Pennsylvanian cotton appliqué bedcover of 1875–1900 was possibly made from a published pattern. While it is in many respects typical of both Pennsylvanian–German arts and central European traditions, the layout, choice of stylized flowers and central shield-breasted eagle (adopted on the Great Seal of the United States in 1784) reflect much more diverse influences.

later English book presses, not of textile artisans themselves. Though intended for amateurs, the imagery and techniques emanating from presses were by the 17th century influencing the professional design and production of textiles. As a result, design became ever more dependent upon rapidly changing styles, which were often gleaned from a range of folios – including those intended for marquetry, stucco work or wood carving – or from imported textiles (see Chapter 6). By the early 19th century, printing had in several ways forever altered the balance of the textile trades (see Chapter 8).

As society became more literate, textiles gradually ceased to be storytelling in the Byzantine tradition, and instead became decorative; after about 1750 monumental tapestries were less and less in demand. It was at about this time that European rural weavers and embroiderers began to hold fast to their evolved traditions, which took on greater symbolic–narrative significance both at home and, as a result, among émigré communities in the Americas. The tradition of inherited textile forms and imagery survived even as urbanization and industrialization appeared. For example, the confronted-animal, 'tree of life' and roundel patterns of Sasanian/Byzantine/Islamic origins were being worked as late as 1900 in Scandinavia and across north- 94 eastern Europe as far as Romanov Russia; they could also be found, little modified, in 19th-century American quilts, woven coverlets and samplers.

Chapter 6: Oriental Influences 1450–1900

The names Ottoman, Persian, Mughal and Ming are all evocative of luxury and splendour. Fine tapestry weaves, boldly patterned silks, velvets and carpets, and striking embroidery are all associated with these cultures, their production sustained within tribal and village cultures, and by feudal systems that survived much longer than those in the West. The continued practice of tribute helped both to finance the manufacture of textiles and to disseminate their styles. Of the four cultures listed above, the first three were Islamic, although the Turkic Ottomans were Sunni, while the Safavid Persians (1502–1736) were Shi'i and Sufi. Thus, the arts of the latter depicted all aspects of life, while those of the former utilized predominantly geometric and stylized plant forms. Those of Mughal India (1526–1858) were indebted to the Persians but were even more naturalistic. Chinese arts, both Ming (1368–1644) and Qing (1645–1911), shared a Mongolian past not only with the Persians, but also with the Mughals, who were descended from Genghis Khan.

The Ottoman dynasty had equally deep roots, emerging just before 1300 as the dominant frontier warriors of northwestern Anatolia, with the Mongolians as their enemies. Nevertheless, earlier Mongolian conquests had dispersed artisans – and with them skills – to those areas of the Balkans that by the mid-15th century were part of the Ottoman empire. (The Ottoman conquest of Constantinople in 1453 consolidated their control of this region.) Between 1514 and 1526 they conquered lands to the east and then to the west, extending their empire from Hungary and the Crimea in the north to the Caspian Sea and the Persian Gulf in the east, and through Syria into Egypt and along the northern African coast as far as Algeria. Importantly, up to the 1770s they controlled trade on the Black Sea and the eastern and southern Mediterranean. By then other invaders had altered the composition of eastern Europe, the Middle East and India. Ethnographers rightly emphasize the multiple layers of influences in these regions, but the most apparent – whether in technique, motifs and their placement, or in garment shapes – owe their survival to Chinese, Ottoman, Safavid and Mughal textiles of 1500–1800. In addition, the mechanisms of taste can be readily seen in their acquisition, imitation and influence, which spanned the globe.

103. With their incongruously scaled naturalistic motifs, Safavid Persian textile designs achieved a sophisticated informality admired and copied ever since. This lavish 17th-century example was woven in silk with silver threads in the ground as well as among the brocading wefts.

The most sought-after and influential Ottoman, Persian and Mughal textiles until the late 17th century were undoubtedly pile carpets. These are classified according to their knots. 'Turkish' knots are symmetrical, while 'Persian' knots are asymmetrical; both types of pile can be of pre-cut lengths or formed from a supplementary weft thread looped up and then cut (or left as a loop as in Nordic rya rugs). Persian knots, which produce a closer texture, were used in Ottoman court carpets, in India and (with some exceptions) in Persia. Both types are worked around two warp threads, while a third type, the 'Spanish' knot – so named because of its prevalence there until about 1700 – is knotted around a single warp. All three types have early precedents, the first two in examples found in the Scythian kurgans of 500–400 BC, and the latter in pieces from Chinese Turkestan dated to the 2nd–6th centuries. The Spanish knot is also found in the handful of early German examples (1175–1225). Few carpets, however, survive from these earlier periods.

Carpet techniques were first introduced to Spain by the Moors in the 700s, and by the 13th century production there was highly developed, with most examples remaining true to the region's Islamic past and employing Turkish patterns. Early examples found in Egypt also have *tiraz*-like inscriptions, and among all the 15th-century carpets exhibiting Turkish and Hispano-Moresque designs derived from 14th-century Chinese damask patterns, only those made in Spain (and also found in Egypt) incorporate Chinese *calligraphy*. However, large-scale ogee patterns, made popular by Italian silk- and velvet-weaving centres, were adopted after about 1425. While elsewhere in Europe the ground often included hemp, Spanish carpets were entirely wool, and increasingly the long, thick high-quality fleece of the merino sheep (which overtook the English breeds as the most sought after). Although Spain's textile production was damaged by the expulsion of Moors and Jews in 1492 (possibly as many as 800,000, many of whom benefited Morocco), Moors skilled in dyeing and knotting remained, particularly in Murcia. This was the main western European carpet-weaving centre until the early 17th century, when the last Moors were deported. Thereafter Spanish production was concentrated in Madrid, which had both tapestry and carpet-weaving workshops.

While the literature on Turkish carpets is immense, few are documented within the region itself until the 19th century, when the Ottoman empire had already been reduced by Persian, Austrian, Polish and Russian conquests. Attempts have been

104. Originating in the southwesternmost part of the Ottoman (Turkish) empire, this 18th-century Algerian silk-embroidered cotton curtain or head scarf reflects a rich blend of influences. While the asymmetrical serrated-edge plant forms are typically Ottoman (though indebted to Sino-Mongolian designs), those clustered into an ogee shape around a central palmette reflect earlier Italian–Islamic exchanges.

105. Many now-classic Turkish carpet patterns were produced in Spain, including those called 'large Holbeins', shown here in a symmetrically knotted all-wool carpet made in 16th-century Anatolia.

106. This Persian silk hunting carpet of 1525–50 has been in the possession of the Swedish royal family since 1655. It displays the large central medallion and quartered inner corners characteristic of many Persian, Mughal and Ottoman court carpets (and frequently copied since as a general format).

made to assign certain patterns to individual Turkoman tribes or settlements, but these often contradict the constructional evidence. Furthermore, under Ottoman law, one-fifth of all conquered peoples (including Persians and Mamluks) were taken as slaves; these were sent to workshops or to become soldiers, until they received manumission. Inevitably, those taken included many carpet weavers, as well as other textile artisans, and so Ottoman court carpet patterns became widely made both in Turkish-knotted carpets and in other techniques. The finest Persian carpets, on the other hand, can be distinguished by their silk piles inlaid with brocaded metal threads. Court carpets were made in Cairo, Bursa and Istanbul (formerly Constantinople), which from about 1500 functioned as the centre for carpet trade, including Persian and Turkoman village production. Exports of

107. This late 19th-century Ottoman silk appliqué illustrates the close relationship between flat-worked and pile-woven textiles. The diagonal emphasis and compacted flower heads in the border of this large cover, some 220 centimetres (87 inches) square, can still be found in southeast European embroideries.

pile carpets to the north and the west are documented from the 11th century, but it is only from after 1453 that substantial evidence of their distribution and influence survives.

In the Balkans and eastern Europe, Turkish carpets circulated among aristocratic and mercantile classes into the 1700s, while Persian carpets were much rarer and far more expensive. In response to the demand, as early as 1456 Moldavian merchants were seeking trade concessions in Istanbul. As was the case in western Europe, these carpets were used on walls, tables and beds, and only rarely on floors. However, eastern Europe also had plentiful imports of carpets of felted camel hair or wool, as well as flat-weave kelim, and, after about 1600, mosaic-work carpets. The latter were related to the embroidered broadcloth inset appliqué work on Ottoman and Persian tents and saddlecloths, now called 'Resht work' after a well-known Persian centre of production in the 19th century. Mosaic-style Transylvanian–Hungarian knotted pile carpets, all relatively small, found their way to western Europe and North America during the 17th, 18th and 19th centuries.

Ottoman kelim were soon imitated throughout European Ottoman states and in fact are still made in some areas to the

108, 109. Flat-woven carpets are generally called 'kelim' and are often constructed in the slit tapestry technique seen in this large Shahsavan bag (109, left). However, various soumak or weft-wrapping techniques (109, centre) were also used over a wide area, although they remained particularly associated with the eastern Caucasus. The surface of a Moroccan 18th-century silk-embroidered linen (109, right), also resembles weft-wrapping, but was in fact worked with close-counted herringbone stitches. These techniques favour a simplification of motifs into highly geometricized forms, a tendency found in many weft-patterned weaves, including eastern European brocaded linen gauzes (108).

present day. The Ottoman style continued to dominate the various kelim designs found in Transylvania, southern Hungary, Moldavia, Bucovina, Bessarabia and the entire Balkans; bags, aprons and skirts in these regions also display Turkish and Caucasian kelim influences. The same is true in Poland and the Ukraine, both of which played major roles in the onward transmission of Eastern carpets to the north and west from the 13th and 14th centuries respectively. Armenian merchants from Persia and Turkey resided in both regions and, after the closure of the Black Sea to Genoese merchants in 1475, began to trade directly with Persia as well as Istanbul. There are 15th- and 16th-century written accounts of local production of kelim, but the earliest surviving examples date from the 1600s.

In western Europe the occasional importation of Middle Eastern (and then later Spanish) carpets is recorded from the time of the Crusades onwards, but knotted pile carpets remained rarities even after their production began in Tournai during the 1400s and in Antwerp during the 1500s. Calvinist weavers fleeing from these cities introduced the technique to Ireland by 1525, and to England some fifty years later. In these countries it was known as 'Turkey work', 'setwork' or 'Norwich work', the

110. This knotted wool on hemp carpet was made in England or possibly Flanders in about 1585, the 'Lotto' pattern being closely copied from a Turkish model.

latter name coming from an important East Anglian centre for figured worsted weaving. Only a dozen English pile carpets survive from pre-1700 but many more pieces of Turkey work exist as upholstery and cushions. (This alternative has been the fate of many worn carpets throughout the ages.) The production of knotted pile carpets was curtailed in the Low Countries and in Britain by the civil wars of the 17th century, but Turkish carpets continued to be imported. Indo–Persian carpets now also became available, initially through Portugal and then via the East India Companies established by the British (1600–1873), Dutch (1602–1799) and French (1664–1789), which imported all manner of textiles.

Indo–Persian carpets were made in several parts of Mughal India, including Lahore (now Pakistan) and Agra, from 1580 to the 19th century, and imitated in Europe by the 17th century.

111. The carnation and cloud-edged palmette designs in this 17th-century Ottoman silk and metal-thread brocaded cloth are indebted to Persia and China respectively. Such motifs also occur in Mughal textiles, but the stately formality of the meandering vine is a typically Ottoman device, and one that was revived in late 19th-century western European design.

Their designs were derived from Persian carpets made in and around Herat and, like Persian silks, employed palmettes, sinuous vines and hunting scenes. Some have stylized serpentine cloud motifs borrowed from the Chinese, a device also seen in cruder form in the borders of some Turkish and Spanish carpets of the 17th and 18th centuries. The earlier impact of Chinese cloud damasks has already been noted, and this type of design had a long life. It was used in Chinese velvets (a technique introduced to Japan about 1600) and up to the early 20th century in Tibetan pile rugs. Similarly indebted to the Far East or central Asia is the palmette motif or *hatayi* often found on Ottoman carpets, silks and embroideries, its name a derivation of *Hatay* (Cathay). Parallels can even be drawn between 'Holbein' or 'Lotto' patterns (see p. 120) and saddle covers and carpets depicted in 13th-century Chinese paintings, and such patterns continued to be made in Chinese Turkestan into modern times. Carpet weaving spread through China itself during the 17th and 18th centuries, initially using the same Turkestan style.

112

112. Pile techniques were not just used for carpets. An important and long-lasting alternative use was in saddle rugs. This early 20th-century Tibetan example, only 64 centimetres (25 inches) wide, incorporates Buddhist lions and, in its borders, Chinese dragons.

As for names, Turkish carpet patterns originating in the 15th century were so often depicted in European portraits that four are known by the names of painters. 'Lotto' (after Lorenzo Lotto, 1480–1556) is an arabesque pattern, while the three geometric patterns named 'Holbeins' (after Hans Holbein the Younger, c. 1497–1543) incorporate large or small octagons or eight-pointed stars. 'Small Holbeins' show further borrowing from the Chinese, in this case outlines of interlaced loops from the endless-knot motif. Ushak, in western Anatolia, was a major carpet-weaving area from at least the 1500s, and the Ushak 'medallion' carpet similarly has stylized blossoms and leaves that relate to Chinese textiles. This design, the 'star' Ushak carpet and a third type known from the 1600s and employing large palmettes and leaves, were exported in large numbers from Smyrna (Izmir), one of two ports (the other was Aleppo) in which between 1581 and 1821 the British Levant Company and its French counterpart had warehouses. All these various patterns and motifs inspired European production, not only of pile carpets, but also of embroidered table carpets, which dominated Portuguese carpet manufacture and were also often made in England. Of these, the 'medallion' and 'palmette' patterns have been frequently copied in carpets made in Spain, France, England, Ireland and the United States from the 18th century to the present day.

113. Between the 1680s and 1720s, the designs of West Caspian silk-embroidered kerchiefs or covers were derived from a combination of contemporary star medallion carpet patterns and 'hooked' cartouches from earlier Tabriz carpets. Such kerchiefs were made by Caucasians, Armenians or Persians in the Persian 'free trade' area through which Chinese, Tartars, Kamluks and Russians traded until the mid-18th century.

In France, knotted pile carpets began to be made in Parisian workshops in 1604. In 1673 these became the crown workshops of the Savonnerie, which was itself merged with the Gobelins in 1826 and continues in operation today. With the decline in demand for tapestries, the various Aubusson workshops also began to make pile carpets from 1743, and by the 1770s the tapestry looms there were also producing flat-woven carpets, as by the 1780s were those of Beauvais. During the same period, and inspired by the Savonnerie, knotted pile carpet-making was revived in England and Belgium, and introduced into Sweden. With the exception of the Savonnerie carpets themselves, which from the 1640s have floral motifs and from the 1660s Baroque strapwork-bounded designs (like those of contemporary appliqué), the majority of carpets produced in northern Europe from the 15th to mid-18th centuries follow Muslim patterns. For 125 years thereafter, European fashions became prevalent

114. This early 18th-century Transylvanian pile carpet, which measures 124 x 164 centimetres (49 x 64 inches), is of the type made from the 1500s to the present day in Hungary and parts of Romania. They were widely exported, and not long after this example was made, border patterns from such pieces began to be reproduced in English Axminster carpets.

but never entirely ousted the established patterns. In England, for example, Axminster output included the 'palmette' Ushaks from about 1750 to 1835. Displays at the 1851 Great Exhibition in London, and subsequent exhibitions, led to their rediscovery by artists, designers and the cognoscenti, and thus renewed imports and indigenous production after Middle Eastern styles. Other types of textiles were similarly influenced.

Turkish carpet designs were also being copied by Flemish drawloom weavers in the 1500s if not before. Tournai became a major centre for worsted-faced lightweight narrow carpet strips (called moquettes), which were – and are still – also used as upholstery. However, because the cut and uncut loops in these are created with a supplementary warp (like velvet), the colours were limited, and their groupings often form a faint stripe. The technique was introduced into Britain and, in the mid-17th century, into France. In England moquettes evolved a compound warp (eliminating the apparent stripe) and became known as 'Wilton' if cut and 'Brussels' if looped. Loom-woven, flat-weave doublecloth and triplecloth carpet strips also have the same characteristic stripe (plain or patterned) and are called 'ingrain', 'Venetian', 'Scotch' or 'Kidderminster' (the last two names indicating later British centres of manufacture).

An entirely separate tradition (although perhaps with ancient connections to the fleece-like piles found in prehistoric eastern sites) is that of the Nordic rya rug. Used originally pile downwards on beds (for which function the English words 'rug' or 'rugg' were restricted until the late 18th century), these are well documented in Sweden and Finland from the late 14th century. Until the 18th century their decoration was primarily on the flat side, with simple patterns created by variously coloured wefts. They were made on the estates of nobles and yeoman farmers, as well as by the Brigittine order, in sufficient numbers to allow their export to Germany and use throughout the British Isles. In all probability these and Turkey work inspired the canvas-based hooked, prodded and needle-looped hearth and bed rugs widely made in rural areas in Britain and North America well into the 20th century. In all cases, even when the design is not of Ottoman or Persian origins, the very concept of using these textiles on the floor came from the Middle East.

The distribution of other Eastern textiles followed similar paths, although only a few of their patterns enjoyed an equally long life in the West. Among these were the bold patterns made popular by southern European weavers between around 1425

115

and 1550 and indebted to Eastern sources for their ogee and meander patterns, as well as their stylized floral motifs such as the pomegranate, carnation and tulip.

Until the 17th century all silk cocoons, threads and fabrics passing through Ottoman territory – including those from Syria, Egypt, Iran, Persia and China – went to Bursa to be weighed and taxed. Located in the major Anatolian silk-weaving and sericulture region, Bursa itself was recorded in 1504 as having one thousand looms weaving ninety types of luxury silks, from satins to velvets, the latter using Italian techniques and patterns to compete with Genoese, Milanese and Florentine velvets (which from about 1450 to 1500 had been imported into Turkey in great quantity). Production at Bursa was so great that it was in near-constant conflict with Persia over additional supplies of raw silk. Although it lost its pivotal place in the silk trade in the late 1600s (due to an outbreak of plague and competition from newer palace workshops), Bursa and the surrounding area remained important until about 1860, particularly for sericulture. During the 1500s, merchants seeking both Ottoman and Persian silks dealt with Bursa, and trade with Russia was extensive. The Tsar monopolized this trade, which sent both raw and finished silks to Finland, Sweden, Britain and Holland.

116. The carnations and tulips on this Turkish linen bath towel of about 1800 were worked in silk and silver thread. The embroidery includes double-running or 'Holbein' stitch. The influence of such patterns was widespread and often symbolic of their nomadic origins. Simplified variations in metal threads can be found earlier on Ottoman velvet saddles, and later in tooled leather saddlery across the Americas.

117. This Chinese silk damask in late Ming style is a reminder of the direct trade between China and Russia. One of a number to be used in Russian flags between 1650 and 1700, it was taken as booty by the Swedish army in the early 18th century.

Between about 1595 and 1629, the Safavids also attempted to monopolize silk trade and production, though with less success. Capitalizing on a victory over the Ottomans and the conquest of Georgia, Azerbaijan, Armenia, Herat and Meshad (and thus of the Ottoman silk-producing regions in the southern Caspian), they established Armenian merchants in the area and took one-third of reeled silks as a form of tribute. By 1600 silk processing and weaving was by far the largest occupation and source of Safavid state income; about one-sixth of state expenditure was on the royal workshops, which made carpets, a range of cloths (including voided velvets, influencing those of Mughal India) and embroideries for both the court and export. The Ottomans responded by placing an embargo on Persian silks, which in turn led to new Persian trading routes that circumvented Ottoman territory. In the 17th century Moscow thus had to have separate trading areas for Persian, Indian and 'Greek' (Ottoman) merchants, who also dealt in pile carpets. After about 1650, Russia also traded directly with China, thus providing Europe with a rich array of luxury textiles. Its trade was most active with western Nordic neighbours, where Russian, Persian and Armenian merchants had warehouses, but raw silk transported from China through Russia also sustained many small 17th- and 18th-century silk-weaving ventures in the German Rhineland, Vienna, Denmark and elsewhere, supplementing supplies that came via sea routes from Turkey, India and China.

The novelty-hungry West adopted and adapted textile and garment forms from all these Eastern cultures. These were often combined indiscriminately, since exoticism rather than authenticity was the goal. In England, for example, where the deep oval neckline of an Ottoman kaftan-type woman's coat was fashionable between the 1590s and the 1620s for masques and informal dress, it was invariably incorporated into a garment embroidered with birds, beasts and coiling floral stems, derived from Persian prototypes. The same patterns were found on contemporary coifs and other small items, and in embroidered and pile

118, 119. A comparison between the portrait of an English lady (facing page) of about 1620, and an 1870s Ottoman skirt and bodice (this page) shows the extent to which English informal and masque dress was orientalized, and the longevity of certain garment forms and their decoration. The lady's embroidered sash is a Persian-style precursor of the woven Kashmir shawls fashionable some 150 years later, while the Ottoman costume, with its silk satin ground worked in couched gilt threads, tinsel and paillettes, represents the preservation of the bullion-work skills for which the region was long renowned.

carpets, while the neckline itself survives in Bulgarian regional dress. Throughout formerly Ottoman Europe similar survivals are common, both in garments and embroidery motifs. Male costume also became orientalized in western Europe in the 17th and 18th centuries, during which time elaborate stripes, 'bizarre' silks and innumerable Chinoiserie designs were similar amalgams of Chinese, Persian and Mughal influences. Such mixtures fed back to these regions, especially India. Between around 1660 and 1800, Indian tambour work reflects Persian, Chinese and Western influences, sometimes the result of immigration; so, the saris preferred by Parsi women were decorated with 'Chinai work', embroidery by the Chinese settled at Surat in Gujarat. Male dress was more overtly orientalized in European Russia, the Ukraine and Poland, where the waist sash or 'Turkish towel' (to which the Iberian and Latin American forms are related) remained an aspect of regional dress, embroidered or woven at each end with asymmetrical floral sprays, long after it had ceased to be fashionable. For late 18th-century European women, this was also *the* exotic accessory in the form of the cashmere shawl.

120

120. With its beast-inhabited garden-like ground, this Mughal tambour-work bedcover, made entirely of silk, reflects Persian influences. It was made for the Portuguese market in about 1680, and includes personifications of the Five Senses.

121. Said to duplicate one owned by Martha Washington, this late 18th-century Kashmiri shawl is typical of indigenous shawl-sashes in its restriction of twill-tapestry decoration to the ends and narrow borders. However, its motifs and its length (275 centimetres/108 inches) have been modified better to suit Western tastes.

The design of cashmere shawls and 'Turkish towels' originated in Persia, where they were a principal product of the silk looms of 16th- and 17th-century Kashan. Both were some 4– 5 metres (13–16 feet) long and 60 centimetres (24 inches) wide, and the finest had gold- or silver-thread grounds. They became so universally desirable that in the 18th century, Armenian merchants arranged for their production in Istanbul, Russia and Poland, and Persian patterns were introduced into the brocaded *patka* of Mughal India. There, the sash/shawl (*palla*) was also assembled from cashmere cloth and twill-tapestry decorative borders, as fine in their texture as the silk *kesi* of China (now similarly used in garment cloths rather than for pictorial panels as they had been previously). The closely related *palla/kesi* weave is thought to have been introduced into India from central Asia and Persia between about 1450 and 1500. (It was also known among Prehistoric Southwest weavers.) Kashmiri border motifs became more abstract after Sunni Afghan conquests in 1753 and then more elaborate following the Sikh invasions in 1819, when 15,000 *palla* looms were recorded. The resulting condensed *buta* (flowers) became widely used in all manner of textiles over the next seventy-five years. In Persia – which had also been overrun mid-century – such designs were adopted in the first decades of the Qajar dynasty (1779–1925) and, although declining at times in the 19th century, by 1900 some 3,000 shawl looms remained in use in Kirman. By this time, here and in Kashmir, shawls were woven with continuous wefts in an effort to compete with European imitators, who had modified the shawl's pattern and shape, from sash-like to square, to create the famous 'Paisley' shawl (named after a Scottish weaving centre, although high-quality variants were also woven in Edinburgh, Norwich, Paris, Russia and elsewhere). By 1900, these and other 'exotic' shawls were more often printed or embroidered than woven, and so common that they were fashionable only for piano or bed throws.

The development and fate of shawl patterns is well charted, as is the European influence upon them. It is typical of a cycle of events that occurs throughout the history of textiles: a desirable pattern or product is imitated by another region, which either uses a more efficient technique in order to reduce the cost or creates new, more fashionable, designs. This in turn affects the originators, who, in order not to lose their position as the principal suppliers of that type of cloth, adopt the new techniques or style. Lesser known examples of this cycle between about 1780 and 1900 are the Lyonnaise silks made especially for the Ottoman market, and the French worsted and silk figured cloths made in imitation of those from Norwich. These, with their vibrant colours and often orientalist carpet- and shawl-like designs, sold well in Spain and her colonies in the Americas, a market that France hoped to control. This practice became particularly prevalent with printed and woven cottons, to India's loss (see Chapter 8). Such competition had less impact on embroidery, even when mechanization was applied in the 19th century, since the technique was so often the mainstay of rural textile production, and not so immediately threatened by international marketing. An example is the embroidery of Tashkent, Samarkand and Bokhara, which changed little after the 18th century. Another factor prolonging the life of designs was the emerging sense of national identity. The Qajar dynasty, for example, consciously revived Safavid carpet, silk and embroidery designs in order to emphasize their re-establishment of the 'old order'.

Throughout the former Ottoman lands there remained a rich visual vocabulary, often shared over a wide expanse. Embroideries of the Greek Islands, for example, are occasionally confused with those of Fez, in Morocco. In northern Africa the Islamic inheritance is apparent in the horizontal ground looms, essentially the same as those used throughout the Middle East. A design vocabulary is also shared, although northern African patterns are typically more geometric, reflecting intertwined Ottoman, Hispano-Moresque and Mamluk influences (which are also widespread in former Spanish colonies). In embroidery, these influences also seem to have played an important role throughout Europe during the 16th century, when the new printed pattern-books contained narrow bands and motifs (as found on Mamluk samplers of between 1171 and 1517) described as to be worked in the double-running stitch known as 'Spanish' or 'Holbein'. Other characteristic Mamluk stitches were pattern darning and close-counted herringbone.

122. Silk-embroidered linen curtains such as this were made by Uzbeks and Tadjiks in western Turkestan, where the trading route to China passed through Bokhara, Samarkand and Tashkent. Typically some 2 metres (7 feet) high, they were also sometimes made in western Ottoman provincial centres.

123. 'Sultan' was the appropriate name given to this silk tissue designed in England by Owen Jones (1809–74) and woven by Warner, Sillett & Ramm in 1870. The undertones of machismo in the Islamic patterns made them suitable for gentlemen's quarters such as smoking and billiard rooms.

Such counted-thread stitches and their patterns, especially decorative bands and paired birds between stylized trees, became and remained the mainstay for samplers and ornamental towel ends (whether decorated with supplementary wefts, printing or embroidery) across Ottoman territories, in Europe and, by extension, throughout the Americas. The same geometric patterns also characterize much knitting, whether Mamluk or Indian, made by the Hazara of central Afghanistan or the Sarakat nomads in northern Greece, or from Bulgaria, Bolivia or the Fair Isles in northern Scotland. Their initial circulation may well be the result of the pre-1475 Genoese trade with Spain and the Armenians via the Caspian Sea; their subsequent impact was undoubtedly due to Spanish colonial expansion and Italian, German and English pattern books. These additionally contained Persian motifs, including those used in Elizabethan and Jacobean coiling stem designs.

Although Spain is broadly acknowledged as introducing the treadle loom, plain knitting and weft-faced plain weaves to cultures such as the Pueblo during the 17th century, its role as a conduit for Islamic influences has yet to be fully explored. Spain's rich tradition of knitting, silk weaving, embroidery and carpet-making was influential in the European courts with which it had extensive contact, whether through Habsburg monarchs or royal marriages. Lost amid the fashions for the Baroque and Rococo, the Iberian visual vocabulary – which often encapsulated the Arab gift for mathematics – was restored by antiquarian publications. Among the earliest of these were studies of Granada's mosaic-laden Alhambra, the earliest important Islamic building (1238–1358) to be rediscovered by Westerners, in about 1800. At the same time Mughal architecture was arousing scholarly interest, although for textile designers this was familiar territory. With the introduction of colour-lithographic plates in the 1830s, it was the Alhambresque style that had the greater impact until about 1870, informing the bold outlines and palette of widely revived medieval patterns. The most comprehensive study, *Plans, Elevations, Sections and Details of the Alhambra*, published by Owen Jones from 1836 to 1845, contained colour plates that profoundly influenced pattern design as well as British architectural ornament.

Jones's seminal *Grammar of Ornament* (1856) illustrated patterns from numerous other cultures and paved the way for a succession of full-colour volumes of designs. Many of these for the remainder of the century focused, like Jones's own work, on

124. This detail of a 1580 – 1620 Italian knitted jerkin gives an indication of the rich effect obtained by working with fine silk and gold threads. The visual liveliness derived from juxtaposing various decorative bands is typical of many counted-stitch techniques, whether knitted, embroidered or added as supplementary wefts.

125. A 1762 Spanish silk-stitched linen sampler preserves designs reminiscent of Renaissance pattern books and subsequent domestic embroidery throughout Islamic countries and Latin America. The fretted diamond forms are found as early as 1200 in Mamluk samplers.

arts of the 'oriental' and antique worlds. However, Jones himself was not a historicist. From 1835 he argued that architectural developments should reflect contemporary culture, and in his *Grammar*, he defined his belief that ornament should be studied for its guiding principles rather than as an exercise in copying. During the 1860s, when Japan ended its near-complete exclusion of foreigners, one result was the crystallization of the Aesthetic Movement, which was expressed in Western textiles through the adoption of entire patterns, individual motifs – including indiscriminate use of *yūsoku* – and 'sad' tones of yellow and olive green. As the influence of Islamic and Japanese designs demonstrates so clearly, in matters of taste and the trade flowing from it, both continuity and periods of obscurity have equal roles to play. Only loss allows rediscovery.

190

Chapter 7: Surface Patterning from Indigo to Ikat 600–1900

All constructed textiles share one feature: their design derives from the direct manipulation of threads, whether dyed or undyed, woven, knotted or individually wrapped, twisted, plaited or embroidered in place. Painting, pattern dyeing and printing begin from a different perspective. Their fundamental impact is visual rather than structural: they are a response *to* the medium rather than the basis *of* it. The nature of the colourant and the method of its delivery to selected areas of cloth are equal partners in this process. Delivery takes two basic forms. The first, known as 'shibori', covers all 'physical' resists such folding, pleating, wrapping and clamping (the latter often around rice, seeds, stones or poles, or between boards). Tie-and-dye (called *bahda* in India and *plangi* among Malay–Indonesian peoples), *tritik* (covering a range of stitch-resist methods) and ikat (in which warp and/or weft threads are bound and dyed prior to weaving) come into this category. The other group of surface-patterning techniques is direct or 'additive'. The cloth is tacked out flat but no real tension is required, eliminating the need for looms or embroidery frames. Fingers, sticks, rudimentary brushes and pens or found objects with a sufficiently prominent surface texture have all been used to make elaborate pictures and complex patterns directly onto cloth, using readily available earth ochres or fruit and vegetable stains. Batik, the use of blocks, and all forms of mechanical printing and embossing are additive and originate from the use of these basic tools.

Like *tritik*, batik and ikat are terms taken from Indonesia, where the patterning of cloths became a primary domestic industry. Until the early 1900s, cloths decorated using these techniques were widely traded by the ruling Dutch, particularly during the governorship of the Dutch East India Company (1602–1798). These and other Indian, Indonesian and Japanese words for pattern dyeing – including the Indian *chitta*, which became 'chintz' – indicate influential areas of production. However, these are not the only regions where surface patterning has had a long history. In 600, indigo additive resist techniques, whether painted or stamped, had also already been in use for at least five to seven centuries in Egypt, Syria, Persia, central Asia, China and Peru, where the coastal Tiahuanaco (500–700)

126. The ultimately global influence of Indian dyeing skills is represented in this western Indian cotton 'kalamkari' from the late 18th century. Each pattern is the result of indigo resist dyeing and stamped mordants: green appeared where blue was overprinted by a mordant for yellow, while the red, purple, brown and black tones developed from different mordants immersed in red dyebaths (including one of alizarin). The white ground patterns had been developed in the previous century, primarily to cater for European tastes.

127. A close look at a fragment of a Japanese silk *kosode* of 1615–1700 reveals a combination of immersion (shibori) and dry patterning techniques in the form of tie-dyeing (used to create the ground colour and the resisted dots) and metallic leaf pressed onto stamped rice paste. Details such as the crane and cloud were worked in silk satin stitches and couched gilt threads.

128. Due to extensive trading, the best known hot-wax resists are those of Indonesia. This central Javanese cotton batik hip wrapper (*kain panjang*) of around 1850 is evidence of the local preference for 'blackened' indigo, here created by overdyeing with a tannin.

129. The Aztec king Nezahualpilli wears a *xiuhtlalpilli tilmatle* (literally, 'blue knotted cloak'). Its tie-dyed 'negative' dots on an indigo-dyed ground are typical of early examples of physical resist patterns found globally, while the border epitomizes the freehand additive-resist 'white line' style.

130. The 'white line' motifs on this rare Huari cotton textile of about 600 (composed of three joined panels) seem to result from a hand-painted resist against an immersion dye. However, given the preference for mineral pigments and tannins in tropical and subtropical regions, the resist could well have protected against directly applied colourants. Discharging could also produce an identical result.

additionally produced highly complex tie-and-dye designs. The Aztecs called their high-status cloaks *xiuhtlalpilli* (indigo resist) and because this type of patterning indicated Toltec descent, physical and additive resists can be dated to Toltec domination of central Mexico between the 10th and 12th centuries.

With the exception of Latin America, wherever there is sufficient evidence to determine cause and effect, the introduction of resist patterning with *any* immersion dye follows in the wake of the trade in Indian resist-dyed cloth or knowledge of indigo dyeing itself. (The introduction of cotton and traded indigo to the southern tribes in the Prehistoric Southwest from Mexico appears to have had the same effect.) This is undoubtedly because, like all photosensitive dyes, indigo patterns must be delivered by a physical or additive resist method. It cannot be positioned outside the dyebath except as 'China blue' or in very small, quickly brushed strokes (the European 'pencilling'), a technique not known until the 1730s. The universal urge to paint, to make a direct mark, combined with the fact that the most straightforward indigo patterning creates 'negative' imagery, resulted in the 'white line' style in which the white resist pattern sits against a dark blue dyed ground. This style

characterizes all known painted and stamped indigo resist cotton, linen and other bast-fibre cloths up to about 950, as well as resists on any other fibre up until about 750.

Already the centre of a multinational sea-trade route that stretched from Egypt to China, India's own indigo production must have been extensive. It is hinted at in the simple indigo-dyed ikat-striped fabrics depicted together with small dot tied-resists in the Ajanta cave paintings of the 4th to 7th centuries. However, prior to the 17th century the Indian skill with indigo can only be appreciated to any degree in the numerous fragments of resist-painted and block-printed cotton export cloths dated mainly between 1200 and 1500 (although the earliest is radiocarbon dated to 870–960) and found in Fustāt, south of Cairo. Indian influence can be seen in the introduction of indigo cultivation, by 100 BC, to the drier parts of southeastern Asia. As cultivation spread northwards during the 4th century, the 'blue and white' style appeared in China, where it became identified with several ethnic groups in the southwest, among them the Miao, who became known as the 'indigo nationality'. Batik – including the use of clamped perforated boards to position the wax – was used on silk for Chinese court consumption and was particularly popular during the Tang Dynasty (618–906). It survives in rural production today, as do cold pastes for printing and stencilling, developed first on hemp and then, from the 11th century, on cotton.

By the 5th century both indigo and writing had reached Japan from China. Because the Japanese word *yūhata* (knotting of

131. In many cultures, expanses of indigo-saturated cloth are still used as a foil for rich decoration. This example was made by a 'White collared' Miao woman, whose arsenal of techniques includes both hot wax and cold paste resists, as well as glazing with egg whites.

132. The silk and gilt-thread embroidery on this Japanese *kosode* of 1800–1850 is enhanced by paste-resisted imagery, the small dots stencilled in imitation of tie-dyeing and the remainder applied freehand. Except for the indigo blue areas, the other colourants were painted directly onto the silk or cold-dyed.

cloth) is native, it may be assumed that at least this type of shibori pre-dates the adoption of Chinese writing. Generally, however, the Japanese use of Chinese characters suggests that many shibori techniques were introduced from the mainland. All early examples are dyed with indigo; in China they are first found among the tombs at Astana (418–683), but after the 9th century the use of shibori appears to die away in this region. Conversely, in Japan it is *rōzome* – the additive brushed-wax resists specifically intended for dyeing – that cannot be traced between 700 and 1900. Their place was taken by shibori, the physical resists, which became highly developed between 1575 and 1700. However, they were themselves undermined when *sarasa* (17th-century imported Indian prints) gave impetus to stencil-resist fabrics that duplicated, with sappanwood and other directly applied dyes, the effect of mordant-printed Indian reds, and often imitated tie-and-dye patterns. On silks, and occasionally hemp, stencilled resists were many-coloured and were often combined with paste resists, freely painted dyes and embroidery (the latter an embellishment frequently combined with indigo resist cloths, here and elsewhere). Cotton, cultivated in Japan since the early 15th century, remained a vehicle for the 'blue and white' style.

Indigo cultivation, trade and patterning was dispersed extensively with Islam (or more accurately, with the Jewish dyers and merchants within the Muslim world), particularly to northern and western Africa and, by the 13th century, to Spain. It is documented in Africa from the 9th century, first in Arab chronicles and then through some five hundred Tellem garments and fragments from Mali dating up to the 16th century. These are almost entirely embellished with indigo-dyed yarns and include a rare 11th- or 12th-century cotton tie-and-dyed man's coif. By the 1300s tropical indigo was being used in Italy to dye cotton and linen yarns and cloths. Thereafter its importation spread northwards, despite strong resistance from woad growers, whose crop was so extensive that it was an important source of tax revenues in France, Germany and, later, England. Although European woad farming continued into the 1900s, by 1660 demand for indigo was such that Britain was trying to monopolize its trade from the North American colonies.

When imported Indian painted and printed cottons began to stimulate imitations in Europe in the 17th century, the French and, later, English governments responded by banning printing in order to protect their weavers. However, these bans were circumvented in a number of ways. French printers, whose ban

133. Nigeria remains known for its *adire eleko*, or starch-resist patterned cloths. First indigo-dyed to mid-blue, the pattern is then drawn on with palm-leaf ribs or feathers using casava or cornflower boiled in alum. Further immersions in indigo turn the unpainted areas dark blue.

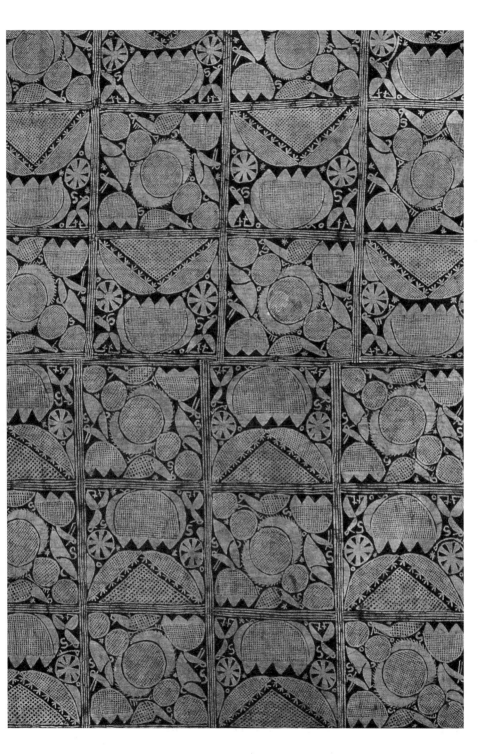

from 1686 to 1759 was the longest, argued successfully that patterns with resisted indigo were not printed but dyed. As a result, French surface-patterning expertise became concentrated on additive resists (other single colours were used apart from indigo). During the same period in central and eastern Europe, including Russia, additive-resist *blaudruck* or 'blue prints' became staple fabrics, block-printed by hand and also, from the mid-19th century to the mid-20th century, by machine. Indigo remained so prevalent in African cloths that those *without* it were noteworthy until modern times. As late as the 1930s half of the population of Abeokuta, the 'Paris of Yorubaland' (in modern-day Nigeria), was involved with indigo in some way. Everywhere there was an unswerving reliance on plain and patterned indigo cloths among tribal and rural cultures, including those of North America. Until 1900 it remained the principal colour of both additive and physical resist techniques, notably *plangi* and *tritik*.

Indigo combined with a red dye is first associated with ikat. The origins of ikat are unknown, but it is easy to imagine how the unravelled cores of a coiled basket – smoke-stained in places, untouched in others – might have suggested this physical resist technique. Yet the earliest surviving examples, found in Japan,

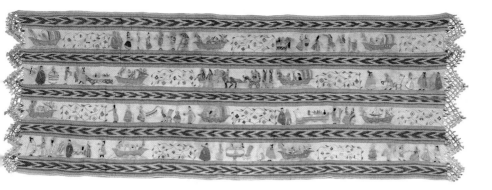

135. Simple warp-ikat stripes are the oldest and the most widely found interpretation of the technique. While they are often the sole decoration, in this late 18th-century Mexican shawl they are combined with embroidered bands.

date only to about AD 600. Those made of silk are thought to have been imported from central Asia, while those of cotton probably came from either India or Yemen – as, in all likelihood, did fragments of cotton ikats dated 650–810 unearthed in southern Israel. Yemeni ikats, which were traded extensively in the Middle Ages, are documented from just before 600, and those surviving from the 9th century were often dyed in indigo and *wars*, a golden yellow. The Japanese and Israeli examples, however, are interesting for the early presence of red with this combination. While the low temperature of the indigo vat and the brief immersions preserve paste or wax resists (whether hand-painted, stencilled or stamped), mordant dyes – especially alizarins – are boiling and thus dissolve such additive resists. Physical resists, in contrast, tolerate high vat temperatures and can be popped into any dyebath: combining indigo and red dyes is thus relatively easy.

Nevertheless, the history of ikats is elusive. By the 1800s they were made in West Africa, the Middle East and all over Asia, as well as at locations scattered throughout Latin America (where they are called *jaspeado*, meaning 'speckled'). Not surprisingly, tie-and-dye techniques were employed on whole cloths in the same areas. (Stitch resists are more specifically associated with Cambodia, Sumatra, Java, Japan and, in western Africa, the Senegal river people.) Weft ikats are associated with Muslim weavers, including those in Indonesia. Double ikats, in which both warp and weft are pre-patterned, emerged in Latin America, Bali, Japan and India. In this last country, *patola* – the all-silk varieties made in western regions and still made in Pattan today – were prized cloths and were made at least as early as the 16th century. The brilliantly coloured and boldly patterned silk warp ikats of Uzbekistan began to be made only a few decades after the revival of silk processing north of Bukara

138

in 1770; their ikat velvets were produced only from about 1850 to 1910. The apparently patchy use of ikat reflects not only changing fashions and fortunes, but the availability of dyes and skills. In the case of full-colour ikats, production required close collaboration between the merchant or client, the warper, the pattern-drawer, two kinds of dyers – those of lukewarm indigo and those of hot mordant colours – and the weaver. When adopted in Europe from the 1700s onwards (where they were called 'chiné'), ikats were therefore only made in urban textile centres. By about 1837, a method of mechanically printing warps (known as 'shadow printing', although some authorities reverse the meanings of this term and chiné) had been perfected. There is also some indication, in Japan at least, that indigo-dyed cotton ikats became more popular during the 19th-century decline of shibori production, which was far more time-consuming even though faster ways to produce the latter, such as pole wrapping, were introduced at this time. Equally, it may be that the simple cotton ikats made there, in Uzbekistan and elsewhere prior to 1800 were used to destruction.

Combining photosensitive-blue and mordant-red immersion dyes was far more difficult on additive-patterned cloths, and it is not seen until the post-1200 Indian examples from Fustāt. The breakthrough came with the recognition that additive resists can be immersed in mordant baths because these are either cold or tepid. It appears that the necessity for resists with indigo led to the concept of resists for mordants and, from there, to the idea of putting the mordant itself into a paste and printing that instead. Using this last method together with additive indigo resists, Indians produced *ajrakh*, the red and blue cottons found in Fustāt. These were painted and block-printed mainly in northwestern India. The southeastern Coromandel coast was known instead for kalamkari, the handpainted – and later block-printed – full-colour cottons. Indian prints became important trade goods, sold not only to Egypt but also to Persia and the Far East, particularly southeastern Asia. They soon began to be tailored to specific markets. During the 1600s, for example, those made for export to Europe gradually gave greater prominence to light grounds (the European preference), a taste transferred back to India and central Asia, where Indian-type block-printing is judged to have begun in the following century.

The particularly common combination of red and black on neutral – found frequently in Indian, central Asian and European block-printed cottons of the 18th and 19th centuries, and

136. One Uzbekistani centre to become synonymous in the 19th century with panels of vivid silk warp ikat was Samarkand, where this example was made soon after 1900. Typically, its motifs are highly simplified and very large: each solar disc is some 44 centimetres (17 inches) across.

137. While the pomegranate-filled 38 centimetre (15 inch) high ogees were inspired by Ottoman woven silks, this 1757–60 French block-printed *indienne ordinaire* (with linen warp and cotton weft) otherwise imitates Indian cottons, both in its red-and-black colour scheme and the small shibori-like dots (*pincôtage*). The delicacy of these and the hatching suggest the hand of a skilled Swiss or German block-cutter.

other cottons such as the ikats of the Deccan and Andhra State in 19th-century India – could be produced with a single immersion in an alizarin dyebath by pre-positioning mordants of alum and iron, respectively. This was an inexpensive method and the French – who, like the Dutch, Portuguese, Germans, Swiss and British, were eagerly seeking knowledge of both full-colour Indian techniques and other 'oriental' printing styles from the 17th century onwards – appropriately called the technique *indienne ordinaire*. Such cloths often had buff-coloured dyed grounds, with variations and details added in a buttercup yellow.

Black, red, tan and off-white can be termed the 'prehistoric palette', distinguished above all else by the absence of any blue, green or purple tones. Even where virtually no textiles survive from before 1800, the antiquity of textile traditions among many ethnic groups in tropical and subtropical zones is testified to by

138. The overdyeing of morinda red and indigo blue to create black is apparent in this Balinese cotton shoulder or breast cloth where the blue alone is revealed in the worn areas (above and below the smallest red star, lower left). The double-ikat pattern is bordered with many bands of gilt counted-thread embroidery. The degree of embellishment indicates that its Tenqanan makers produced it for ceremonial use.

the prominence of this palette and its association with the most auspicious and solemn occasions. In fact, indigo was – and sometimes still is – dyed with a tannin or red to blacken it. Indonesian ikats, for example, were dyed morinda red and indigo, often combined to make a brownish black; their 'blue and whites' were made only as export cloths for the Dutch and Chinese. Medieval wool dyers in Europe produced a similarly prized black, *bruneta*, with woad and madder. This combination (or indigo, woad and yellow weld) set the standard until the introduction from Latin America of logwood for black. The latter became so important to 18th- and 19th-century European wool, linen, cotton and hat manufacturers that the Spanish and British often skirmished over its trade. Indeed, the British colony of Honduras owed its existence to it.

Such colours were either used alone or else were brought together in such little-changed techniques as inset felt, embroidery, coiling and twining. In addition, they are frequently found in the painted illustrative cotton panels depicting religious, mythological or epic tales, from Tibet to the American Prehistoric Southwest. Indeed, all Native North American and Mesoamerican peoples exploited the natural abundance of red,

139. Painted cotton mantles such as this continued to be made and valued by the Muisca (who inhabited the high plains of Colombia from about 600) into the 1600s. Its colours are directly applied, probably around a 'white line' resist, and include a rare example of a blue-green copper sulphate shade.

yellow and buff ochres, iron-laden muds and tree bark and gall-nut tannins. Tellingly, like the Egyptians before them, reds were made from ochre in preference to those just as widely available from alizarin-rich roots. Alizarin was instead mordanted with metallic salts to create dyed browns and blacks.

This 'prehistoric palette' derives from ancient cold patterning techniques. Cold techniques are akin to watercolour and oil painting, as well as ceramic glazing. They encompass all additive surface patterning techniques *except* immersion or steaming. These are also called 'dry' processes, since the critical factor is that the patterning substance, whether pigment, direct dye, mordant, or a colour-altering chemical, soaks into the cloth and dries thoroughly. Chemically it does not matter how the substance is positioned on the cloth, nor whether the imagery is positive or negative. The earliest presently known example, from el-Gebelein, Egypt (4000–3500 BC), is positive, having directly painted funerary and hunting scenes in black, red and white on buff linen. Although on wool, almost identical colours – black, dark red and tan – form the background to pictorial friezes on the earliest examples in negative or 'white line' style as found in Scythian kurgans in the Crimea (450–375 BC). There, resist paste was needed not to prevent colouring during immersion dyeing, but instead to keep different directly applied colours from overlapping, thus allowing very rapid painting while providing crisp-edged imagery. The painted clothing of contemporary Caucasus Mountain tribes to the southeast undoubtedly displayed the same colours, since the Greek historian Herodotus emphasized that the colours were directly applied in liquid form and lasted the lifetime of the garment.

The same combinations of colour and technique remain in use – on body and cloth – among native populations in New Zealand and Australia. In Africa, where stamping of patterns is rare, the well-known Ghanaian *adinkra* cotton cloths are printed in black by the Ashanti using carved calabash pieces. Their pigment comes from tree bark boiled with iron slag. The Baganda of West Africa pattern bark cloth with the most extensive range of designs documented in Africa, using stencils cut from banana leaves. Here, the black pigment is a mixture of vegetable matter and iron-rich mud. Similar pigments were used by the Kuba and pygmy tribes of the Congo (formerly Zaire), who decorated their bark cloths freehand, as did numerous cultures to the west, whose cloths included cotton: the Cameroonian grasslanders, the nearby Nigerian Ibibio, the northern Nigerian Hausa and the Senufo of the Ivory Coast. Climate has not favoured survival of textiles in any of the tropical and sub-tropical regions, precisely where cold techniques were widespread. Although some examples from the early Paracas period onwards illustrate their longevity in South America, few survive to the north. Nevertheless, the Nahuatl name for Aztec men's capes, *ixnextacuilloli* (meaning painting or writing on the surface with ash), suggests that some bore similar traits. Among the very few exceptions to the 'cold' palette are a greenish shade of leaf-and-mud pigment used in the cloths worn by Senufo men of the Poro clan, and the bluish copper sulphate shades found occasionally in the Precolumbian Americas.

The same range of colours associated with cold techniques is used in tapa (bark cloth) patterning. Archaeological and linguistic evidence suggests that this technique, together with some of the necessary plants, arrived in the Pacific Islands some three thousand years ago from southern China and mainland southeastern Asia. The techniques still in use are revealing of ancient practices. The principal colourants (ignoring *loa*, a red seed-dye introduced in the early 1800s) are reddish-brown bark juices (especially *'o'a* from the koka tree), black soot from burnt nuts,

yellow from turmeric roots, and red ochre (a prized but scarce colourant traded throughout these islands). These are applied freehand with a brush with the exception of the red ochre, which is spread as a grated powder and rubbed into the surface with a tapa-wrapped 'brush' dampened with 'o'a. Powdered red ochre is also transferred from a patterned tablet by laying the cloth over it and rubbing with a pad of 'o'a-dipped cloth. Until the last century most tablets were made of robust natural materials sewn to a pandanus leaf, itself tied to a board. This is still done today in Tonga, but has elsewhere been gradually replaced by carved wooden tablets, thought to have originated among the Fiji Islanders (who also used large leaves, such as banana leaves, as stencils for predominantly black patterns). To the east, the Hawaiians, whose original tapa tradition was extinct by 1900, had plentiful supplies of red and yellow ochre. Their vivid colours have been preserved in rare copies of Alexander Shaw's record of Captain Cook's voyages, published in 1787.

'Dry' treatments provided supplements or alternatives to immersion. This was true both where mordant dyes were understood – as in *indienne ordinaire* – and where they were not used, as in Heian Japan (794–1185). There, silks were dotted or rubbed with wax and then rubbed with flower or grass juices (called

140. Cold-dyed patterns – finger painted, ruled with fine pens and multi-pronged liners, and stamped with narrow pattern bands made from carved strips of bamboo – are preserved among the samples of Hawaiian tapa cloths collected by Captain Cook on his third voyage of 1776–79.

141

141. This mid-700s Japanese silk illustrates the use of wax resist with either an immersion dye (*rōzome*) or, more probably, a cold dye (rubbing or brushing prepared plant juices directly into the cloth, known as *rōzuri*). Such cloths were among those accepted as payment of taxes.

rōzuri, essentially *rōzome* wax-resist dyeing adapted to a non-immersion technique). Silks were also patterned with safflower rubbings from carved blocks in a method related to that of the Pacific Islanders. Rubbing was elsewhere long used by many basketmakers to dry-dye twined elements locally, as the work progressed (in concept like ikat). In the West, it was not until the 1730s that the English adapted such techniques to produce 'China blue', in which powdered dye matter (indigo) was suspended in a paste. Cloths thus printed were then immersed in alternate baths of lime, to dissolve the indigo, and ferrous sulphate, to reduce it. This technique finally allowed direct printing with indigo and remained in use until about 1900, after which variations substituted synthetic indigo, isolated by Baeyer in Germany and increasingly available.

Many other pre- and post-submersion forms of patterning have been used since about 600. Two silks from the Han tomb at Mawangdui (168 BC) demonstrate the antiquity of dry-patterning techniques. The first, a gauze, is stamped with gold and silver paste. The other, a tabby weave, is stamped, stencilled and painted in six colours. Since silk readily absorbs dyestuffs, the patterning of this one might have stopped with the application of the colourants, as was certainly the case with the watercolour-

142. There are several ways to produce the colour combination seen in this Chinese silk: in this case the cloth was cold stamped with an alkaline paste, turning the red to yellow. It was originally used to cover a rush floor-mat in the household of Empress Regnant Kōken (749–58).

painted Chinese silks fashionable in Europe in the 18th century. However, dry-dyed silks (and less often wools) were also subjected to a wet after-treatment to render the colours fast. This alternative technique reflects one of the most important uses of cold processes: to position a substance that will either respond to subsequent immersion or else change the colour of an already-dyed cloth. Discharge printing, for example, bleaches out selected areas of dye. One ancient discharging technique is illustrated in the Bambara (Malian) *bogolanfini*, which are cotton strip-cloths (seamed narrow lengths of handwoven fabric) carrying striking white geometric patterns on a black ground. Their decoration begins by washing the cloth in water, drying it in the sun, and dyeing it in a yellow leaf infusion. Next, the background around the pattern is drawn out with year-old pond mud. The mud is dried, washed off and, after another immersion in the dyebath, the background is again drawn and dried. The ore-saturated mud functions both as a mordant, turning the yellow dye to black, and as a resist against an application of a discharge 'soup' of peanuts, caustic soda, millet bran and water, painted into the non-muddied areas. It is left for a week before a final wash, when the discharged yellow disappears, leaving a white background.

Several mid-8th-century silks found in China, near Astana, demonstrate two less labour-intensive uses of strong alkalis such as caustic soda (sodium hydrate). In the first the silk is dyed dark red and then stamped using six-point medallion and bird patterns with a strong alkaline paste, turning those areas yellow. A yellow turmeric or safflower ground treated in the same way would turn to red, an effect seen on many cottons and silks around the world throughout the following centuries (and, in the Napoleonic era, adopted as part of the Western fashion for antiquarian styles). The second use exploits the reaction of the fibre itself to alkalis. Silk left in its natural state is 'gummed'; a stamped alkaline paste bites into the fibre and 'de-gums' it (and eventually destroys it if this action is not stopped by immersion in a mild acid bath). The result is an increase in the absorption of dye in certain areas, thus creating a subtle two-toned pattern. The same principle of 'destructive' printing became fully developed in devoré (French for 'devoured'), the velvets or velveteens with pile and ground weaves of different fibre types. If of silk or wool, the pile could therefore be removed entirely by a destructive alkaline paste, leaving the ground of cotton or linen intact. The late 19th-century chemical laces were patterned using the same principle. As these examples show, there are several means

142

143. Devoré is a 'destructive' technique in which a pattern is created by removing unwanted areas of pile. In this detail of a Liberty scarf, the silk pile was destroyed by printing an alkaline paste, which revealed the viscose cellulose ground cloth. Additional colours were applied by screen-printing the intact pile first.

to the same ends and several ends from the same means. This is so much the case that it can be very difficult to tell the difference between resist and discharge printing, not least because they can be used together on the same cloth.

Histories of Western printing often overlook the long-established and continuous reliance on pigments and localized dry printing techniques – distinguished in the 18th century as 'embossed' prints – even after the European discovery of Indian full-colour immersion techniques in the late 17th century. This underpins the constant European drive to transform Indian wet pattern-dyeing into dry printing. Mineral (inorganic) dyes, developed between 1749 and the 1840s, depended largely on the concept of suspended pigments precipitated directly on the cloth with an often alkaline print paste, dried and then developed by immersion in a chemical bath. Related steam dyes combined all the essentials in the print paste, catalysing them into a localized dye by steaming. Many metallic mordants such as copper (which became important in 17th- and 18th-century Europe) and newly isolated metals such as chromium (discovered in 1797) were reformulated into precipitates in order to provide an ever-increasing range of printer's colours. Greater knowledge of their chemical constituents was intertwined with that of inks, paints and ceramic glazes, all of which made great use of indigo, gallnut, ochres and other ores. The chemistry of carmine acid and alizarin was understood in France by the 1820s when the development of synthetic dyes also began. The mauve isolated in Britain in 1856 by William Perkin was the first to be made from coal tar. Thereafter this was the main source of new synthetic dyes. Developments continued in France, but both countries were eclipsed by the German dye industry, which in terms of dyestuffs and technical support led the world by 1900, rivalled only by the Swiss. These dyes can, with very few exceptions, be applied directly, or cold.

Western printing methods are therefore an amalgam of old skills in cold painting and stamping techniques, Indian methods, and the discovery of tropical and subtropical dyes, whether logwood from old Maya lands or catechu, the traditional Indian brown dye only introduced into Europe in the 1830s. Stealth and bribery often underpinned the acquisition of skills: in the 1780s, for example, the British offered a premium for the 'Turkey red' method, which essentially rendered cottons more like wool or silk by animalizing them with an oil-based mordant (still done in India up to at least 1900 by rubbing with pig fat). From the 17th

144

145

144. A roller-printed cotton, both engraved and printed by the English firm of William Orme, typifies the mineral dye palette of 1820–60. The scene illustrates the Crystal Palace, the centre-piece of the Great Exhibition held in London in 1851.

145. The secret to dyeing cottons with a fast, brilliant alizarin eluded northwestern European printers until the 1780s. Often called 'Turkey [meaning Ottoman] red', its effect can be seen in this 18th-century northern Indian tent panel. The panel was blocked and painted with mordants and resists prior to at least three separate dyeings. Of these, the red dyeing was the most complex.

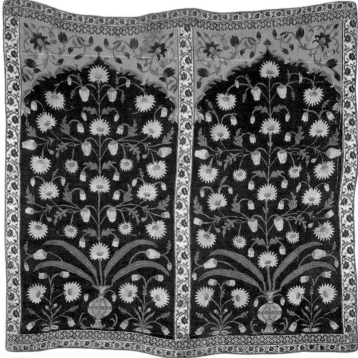

century onwards, the principles and substances which elsewhere had long histories of intuitive use, akin to cooking, were rendered explicable, amendable, reliable and 'dry'. Mainly inorganic, but occasionally organic, these were faster to light and washing than any forerunners except indigo, which always set the standard. European chemists also gradually replaced the most injurious substances – for example, the arsenic in tropical indigo vats, 'China blue', and several notorious greens – with chemicals less toxic though still often noxious. For all the resulting beauty, dyeing was, and is, a dangerous business. Additionally, the understanding of cold patterning underpinned the impact of rotary printing machines, which by about 1828 (in Lancashire, England) could print three colours simultaneously. Together, these developments consolidated the British domination of cotton printing in the global market until about 1900.

146. This English full-coloured glazed cotton, or chintz, of about 1830, exhibits a combination of Western technology (in the roller mordant-printed reds) and ancient non-Western pattern dyeing techniques. The latter appears in the form of the block-printed mordant for quercitron yellow (from the American oak), which together with blue makes the brilliant green. The indigo itself may have been removed where necessary by the acidic discharge process new in the late 1820s.

Chapter 8: The Importance of Cotton and Linen 1500–1950

Until about 1950 plant fibres were always the mainstay of textile production. Among the animal fibres, silk was and remains the most scarce. Even with the introduction of Spanish merino sheep to flocks around the world and the vast increase in wool supplies from Australia and New Zealand after about 1800 and 1850 respectively (at a time when France and her colonies dominated production), wool consumption worldwide was never more than one-quarter that of cotton alone. By the mid-19th century, Western machine-made cotton yarns and cloths were distributed globally alongside specialist hand-printed goods – often eliminating local production in the process. In addition, cotton had replaced linen in many weaves and other textile constructions. It was more difficult than linen to hand spin, but easier to dye, hence cotton's early prevalence as a base-cloth for fast-dye patterned, washable fabrics. Silk, wool and linen were still printed, but as with many other techniques appropriate for any fibre, cotton played an increasingly dominant role. Lace-making, knitting, tatting, crochet, quilting, patchwork, appliqué and many other stitched techniques all fell under its sway.

In examining how cotton became so important among fibres, this chapter begins near the end of the story, with the demise of the old linen industries. Once the cheapest yarn compared to silk, wool and cotton – which traditionally ranked in that order, with silk the most valued – by 1920 linen had become the most expensive: prices were then rising for all fibres, but while those for silk had less than doubled since about 1910, linen had became six times more costly. The Russian Revolution and the First World War had decimated vast areas of flax and hemp cultivation (and, as an aside, slaughtered thousands of horses, thus bringing to an end the widespread use of horsehair). As a result, linen ceased to be the fibre of necessities and niceties. Sheets, tablecloths, towels, handkerchiefs and crisply starched shirts had once exploited its coolness, sheen, wet-strength, washability and smoothness, but by 1950 the term 'lingerie' alone preserved the memory of the finest linens.

In 1500 the cultivation of flax and hemp – both of which were made into cloths called 'linen' – had become highly developed in areas where cotton could not be grown. Until around 1780, linen

147. Swiss laundry maids are churning and bleaching linen cloths in *The Weekly Wash*, embroidered in wool on linen in 1556. By this date Swiss tapestry weaving had declined and been replaced by a form of couching called 'Kloster' or 'convent' stitch after a principal source of such panels.

remained the essential alternative to wool in the northern hemisphere, where it was important both for rural communities and within hand-powered industry. For example, in Scotland (where originally nettle fibres were used) flax yarns and cloths were the only manufactured products for most of the 1700s. Large-scale, high-quality production was initially dominated by Flanders, which supplied the finest plain linens (such as cambric and lawn) as well as figured cloths such as table damasks. It was also responsible for the best bleaching. As with other specialized textile types, the making of such damasks spread in the later 16th century when Protestant weavers moved northwards to escape the religious intolerance of the ruling Spaniards. Holland, especially Haarlem, became the foremost source of luxury linens until similarly motivated emigration after 1685 benefited regions such as Saxony and Ireland. (The Irish industry only became sizeable after about 1750, with the aid of seeds from North America's indigenous flax.) Many linens preserved the names of these centres. Fine tabby-woven cloths were holland, cambric (from Cambrai, now in northern France but then in Flanders) and silesia (lawn from this Austrian–Prussian province); of these, the first was the more expensive because it was heavier. Diapers – the little diamond-based patterns needing multi-harness (or multi-shaft) treadle looms – were from Ypres (d'Ypres), while terms for similar but even coarser flax and hemp cloths such as osnaburg and ticklenburg indicate Prussian–German origins (although these types of textured linens were widely made). By the 15th century, diapers had become the basis for the linen cloths from Perugia, Italy, which, like many linens throughout southern, central and eastern

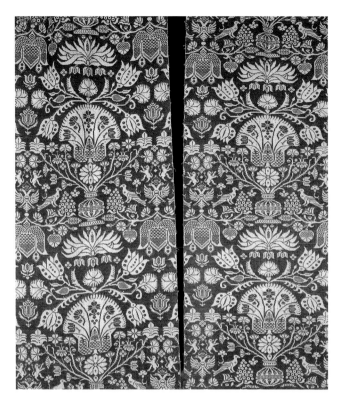

Europe into the mid-20th century, had bands of coloured pattern introduced through the use of supplementary wefts. Aside from yarn-dyed stripes (especially checks or plaids), linen cloths were usually decorated with yarns of other fibres except when the embellishment was itself white.

The decorative potential of linen cloths and yarns continued earlier trends in basts and other plant materials and was derived principally from construction rather than colour. Damasks, which play solely on the juxtaposition of reflective and matte weave structures, are a good example of this. In the absence of silk – the most reflective of fibres – linen provided the next most lustrous surface. Until the early 19th century, damasks could only be woven on drawlooms and so although silk damasks were fairly low in the hierarchy of patterned silk fabrics (being eclipsed by silk velvets, brocades and embroideries), flaxen damasks within the range of linen products were prestigious cloths. The most costly of these were large commemorative or monogrammed tablecloths with their requisites: a dozen napkins, a cupboard cloth and a long towel that accompanied the

149. The colour in this 19th-century Sardinian linen and wool decorative towel or cover is provided entirely by supplementary wefts of wool. Often the trellis-like diaper patterns were woven solely in natural-toned yarns with colour introduced only in the more elaborate end bands.

150. Although generally typical of 17th-century Dutch linen and worsted drawloom-woven cloths, the inclusion of a Prussian-style double-headed eagle in this cloth suggests an origin in Saxony after 1685, when weavers from Holland settled there.

151

151. This linen woven in Holland in the mid-1600s employs a damask weave to illustrate the story of David and Bathsheba. The mirrored sideways repeat typical of drawloom-woven cloths of the period is especially evident in the lettering.

152. *Reticella* was highly developed in Italy by about 1600. Here, the linen band was cut to leave only narrow square grids, which were then filled with patterns worked in buttonhole stitch. All Western needle laces developed from this technique.

finger bowl. (Narrow decorative towels, which typically hung near or on the door, were the vestige of this practice and such towels obtained other widespread ceremonial and symbolic uses.) Linen was not only washable, it could literally take a beating. The harder the washing the more beautiful it became. This happened many times in the lifetime of a linen cloth, whether by pummelling against riverside rocks or 'churning' in a cauldron. Fine table damasks and other household linens were not only subjected to constant washing, but were also refinished on each occasion. This repeated the initial end-treatment, involving bleaching with water made alkaline with ashes, fern or kelp, then an acid bath to neutralize the bleach and much pounding ('beetling') to restore the shine. Both the yarn and cloth had already been thoroughly bleached before purchase (the cloth taking up to six months to whiten). Domestic finishing simply 'topped up' this long process in days, but also included starching to resist soiling and pressing in large screw-clamp devices.

Starching and pressing were widely used techniques, and silks, worsteds and cottons were also glazed and subjected to high-pressure treatments known as 'calendering'. But it was with linen that these treatments were most effective, for it retains creases – as the ancient Egyptian pleated linens demonstrate – and yet when starched and pressed can be rendered stiff and smooth. These last characteristics, together with those of

14

fineness, strength, length and resistance to tangling, were exploited to the full in lacemaking, which emerged around 1500. Lace and lace-like constructions were used around the world, but it was in Europe that the greatest number of forms evolved. True laces are divided into two types. The earliest is needlelace, so called because its basis is a buttonhole stitch. At first used to fill large squares cut out of plain linen cloth (*reticella*), it soon became an independent technique building first flat (*punto in aria*), and then boldly raised, motifs. The starched ruffs and cuffs of 16th- and early 17th-century Europe were composed of *reticella* and *punto in aria* and, as their names imply, these fashions originated in Italian city-states, several of which – notably Milan – were Spanish-ruled until 1714. Next came the northern European response: bobbin lace, a plaiting and twisting technique that used weighted threads (in concept very close to the warp-weighted loom). Flemish and Italian centres, among others, thereafter vied with each other to set the trends and these, too, are preserved in the names for laces, as are many variations. Hardanger, for example, is the Norwegian form of *reticella*.

Even more widely made than laces were the intermediate 'pre-lace' techniques of darned, pulled and drawn threadwork. In the latter two, yarns of a plain linen cloth are bunched and bound into patterns by supplementary threads; in drawn work some yarns are removed altogether. These were the forerunners

157

153. Bobbin lace, as this 1855–60 Belgian linen handkerchief illustrates, is an interlacing technique that can produce solid areas very much like plain-woven cloth. This example of a type called 'Valenciennes' was made in the convent of Notre Dame de la Visitation, Ghent.

154. Composed of 195 alternating squares of cutwork and buratto (each 12.7 centimetres/5 inches across), this Spanish linen cover of 1600–20 displays techniques still worked in Spain and former colonies, but now in cotton. The buratto border illustrates the similarity between darned knotted netting and true laces. Such knotting, especially of fringes, is an echo of Spain's Islamic past.

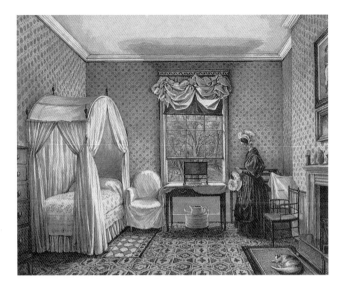

155. All of the white cloths furnishing this English bedroom of about 1835 would have been of cotton, from the muslin tent bed draperies to the Bolton coverlet on the bed. The blind might have been of linen, but otherwise the only certain use of that fibre would have been in the backing for the prodded or hooked hearth rug, seen right, atop an ingrain carpet.

of *reticella* and themselves an extension of darned (or needle-run) patterns, whether worked on solid cloth or on twined or knotted netting. All of these, however, are two-stage construc-tions, comprising the ground cloth or mesh and the subsequent binding or darning stitches. Fifteenth-century Russian linens show the use of coloured other-fibre threads typical of the drawn and pulled work still made in the early 21st century in many rural areas around the world, but the arrival of true laces and their single-stage construction using linen alone heralded a 450-year period during which white linens and laces became power-ful symbols of wealth, propriety and cleanliness.

Whitework – that is, white embellishment on white cloth – was used by all sections of society, the only distinction being the degree of fineness and whiteness. Aside from clothing and in religious contexts, it was most prevalent in bedding and in win-dow curtains. The latter were rare until the 18th century, but by the end of that century white muslin curtains had become fash-ionable. As these became increasingly common, more elaborate variations appeared with lace insertions, needle-run designs, appliqué or, after about 1850, machine-made cotton variations of all these and 'pre-lace' techniques. Colourful bed 'ruggs' gave way to monochrome coverlets worked in damask- and sampler-type designs created by supplementary weft loops or long floats. These were related to true fustians, fabrics such as corduroy and velveteen, which then had a linen warp and prominent cotton weft. ('False' fustians such as jean used the same fibres but simpler weaves, brushed to suggest a richer, fuzzier surface.) Fustians were among the many lighter-weight mixed-fibre cloths originally indebted to Middle Eastern weavers but in the mid- to late 16th century dispersed by émigré Flemish weavers to sympathetic countries such as Britain. There, these so-called 'new draperies' transformed cloth-making. As regions became increasingly specialized, both true and false fustians became centred around Bolton, which gave its name to handwoven all-cotton white coverlets patterned with weft loops.

Bolton coverlets may have been made as early as the 1670s, but it was between the 1760s and the 1850s that exports reached their peak. Needle-run variants were also made. A sizeable cotton whitework industry – adapting according to changing uses and tastes – continued in the region up to about 1950. During the early 1900s, for example, the Bolton cotton mills of Barlow & Jones made not only domestic goods such as 'turkish' (looped-warp pile) towels and fine-quality marsala quilts in imitation of Marseille quilting or *trapunto*, but also white blankets, using waste yarns, that long clothed the majority of native central and southern Africans (who dyed them red). Elsewhere, the pattern-looped coverlets themselves had equally long histories. In Spain these *confites*, with small weft-loops or looser cut and uncut loops, were made from as early as the 1760s until the 1940s, initially using hempen warps and sometimes with blue wool loops rather than white cotton ones. Wherever cotton was grown or imported in quantity, these and similar techniques appeared. Cut-loop types were handmade in the United States, particularly in the southern mountain regions, until these 'candlewick spreads' were replaced by machine-woven versions.

Cotton was thus caught up in the search for white or near-white cloths. Although the pure white cotton boll is now emblematic of this crop, many varieties produced coloured lints. Bleaching was therefore equally time-consuming: 18th-century records from Madras, in southern India, describe a six-month-long process including goat's dung for washing the brown cloth, boiling three times in a starch of congee rice and using indigo to prevent red and brown spots in the congee and cloth. (The blue kernels in modern washing powders are a legacy of the latter.) Well-charted sea routes, pioneered largely by the Portuguese, greatly increased the availability of bleaching materials, as well as of dyes and cotton itself. The marriage in 1662 of Charles II of England to the Portuguese infanta, Catherine of Braganza, had profound consequences for British textile manufacture. Her immense dowry included the ceding of Portuguese trading rights in the East Indies, Bombay, Tangiers and Brazil. Soon, English all-cotton cloths were made with yarns from the latter and the Caribbean Islands. Both remained significant sources of cotton throughout the 18th century.

With additional supplies from the Ottoman Balkans and the Levant, European cotton industries grew in importance. As well as Dutch, British and French centres, the Swiss town of Neuchâtel was known for textile printing, and Switzerland in general for cotton cloths and their trade. Aside from raw materials, Spain imported vast quantities of textiles from its Latin American colonies. The impact of this remains unexplored, but is suggested in the apparently subsequent production, both rural and professional (the latter based in Catalonia), of many varieties of cotton gauze weaves. In return, Spain shared with the colonies its considerable expertise in whitework. North American crops only became important exports in about 1805, when the introduction (some twelve years after its invention) of Eli Whitney's mechanical gin for removing cotton seeds coincided with the destabilization of Europe. Even after the end of the Napoleonic wars in 1815, central Europe and Spain had little peace – or industrialization – until the 1870s. This gave a lead to Britain, then to the United States, and finally to Russia.

Despite innovations elsewhere, until about 1820 the Indian subcontinent remained the world's greatest producer of luxury

finished cotton textiles, distributed by their own traders as well as by the Dutch, Portuguese and, especially after 1600, the British. Until the 1780s there were also several critical differences between the Indian cloths and the cottons made elsewhere, not least the superior strength and fineness of Indian hand-spun yarns. These qualities could be attributed to the retention of the spindle, which was used, for example, in the most sought-after muslins, made in the Dacca (Dhaka) district in eastern Bengal (an area that was naturally endowed with a finer variety of cotton than that grown elsewhere on the subcontinent). Except for English highly twisted fine worsted yarns, European spinners had by the 16th century almost universally adopted one of two spinning wheels – large for discontinuous bast-fibre spinning, small for continuous woollen spinning – and could not yet produce a cotton yarn strong enough to be used as a warp. Their 'cottons' were thus really linen-warp, cotton-weft cloths, unless imported yarn or cloth itself was used. For example, the Jouy-en-Josas printworks, founded in France by Christophe Oberkampf in 1760, used Indian cotton cloths sporadically from 1767 and consistently for the twenty years after 1776.

Indian muslins were in particular demand from 1700 to 1820, being the basis of the finest of drawn and pulled threadwork, called 'Dresden work'. (A speciality of Denmark and northern Germany, Dresden work descended from the Baltic tradition but was all white, extraordinarily soft and intricately darned.) The cloth's handle depended entirely on the yarn, which was so fine that in the 1790s one length of Dacca 'superfine' muslin took a head weaver, weaver and journeyman six months to produce.

By that time, however, the yarns were mainly British. This shift can also be seen in the establishment, with the help of an Italian émigré, of a Scottish sewn-muslin industry in the Edinburgh region during the early 1780s, which mushroomed to the west in Ayrshire using locally made cotton yarns and cloths.

The innovation propelling these changes was the introduction of machine spinning in England. The earliest known attempt to group spindles together in a frame was patented in 1678, while mechanical power was applied to a single wheel during the 1730s. The first successful hand-powered multi-spindle machine, based on the large-wheel principle, was James Hargreaves's 'jenny' (*c.* 1764), but its threads were coarse and too weak for warps. Within five years waterpower was applied to small-wheel type continuous spinning (Richard Arkwright's water frame), producing a coarse thread strong enough for a warp. Meanwhile, advances had been made in fibre preparation processes. Combining aspects of the jenny and water frame (and thus named a 'mule'), Samuel Compton's 1779 patent finally provided fine, strong threads. Within a decade or so, water- and steam-powered spinning was common and machine-spun yarns were being distributed globally to handweavers. In Britain these yarns revolutionized hand-frame knitting and made a substantial contribution to the machine-making of nets and laces (see Chapter 9). However, many formerly prosperous linen weavers

158. The delicacy of this pattern, block-printed in England by John Woolmer in 1775–80, is apparent because the ground is a fine all-cotton cloth. The warp either came from India or else was an early example of English 'mule' spinning. The design was derived from the 'chinoiserie' engravings of the Frenchman Jean Pillement (1719–1808).

159. China had cotton machine-spinning mills by the 1890s, about the time that this child's 'nonofficial' (or informal) waistcoat was made from plain-woven dyed cotton cloths. Its decoration was worked in silk straight and filling stitches, with laid and couched gilt threads.

were reduced to poverty. (Hand-spinning was never lucrative and the 'breaking' of flax and hemp fibres and weaving of sacking was already an occupation for workhouse and prison inmates.)

Cotton-spinning technology was quickly acquired by North America, even though the emigration ban on skilled British artisans was not repealed until 1824. Within four years a patent in the United States for ring-spinning resulted in the stronger but coarser threads that remained the mainstay of North American spinning into the 1900s. In England, Edmund Cartwright's experiments with the power-weaving of plain cloths, begun during the late 1780s, were still being perfected in 1820 but followed in the wake of factory spinning as it spread around the world thereafter. For example, from the 1850s there were modern cotton mills in Brazil, employing immigrant skills and entrepreneurs from Britain and the United States, and by the 1890s industrial cotton-spinning factories in China, some of which were financed by the British and Japanese.

160. Often with large orientalized patterns drawn by professionals for embroidering at home, crewelwork got its name from its worsted, or crewel, yarns. For bed-hangings like this English example of 1675–1700, the ground cloth was usually a linen-warp, cotton-weft jean, a term by the mid-19th century applied to an all-cotton twilled cloth.

It is no coincidence that the first century in which there was an abundance of machine-spun cottons also saw the revival of off-loom techniques. Professional makers of lace, fringe, tape and tassels quickly adopted cotton, in the process making these items much more widely available. Beginning in the 1820s, skilled amateurs aided by an increasing number of 'ladies' books' and magazines (and later booklets printed by the yarn companies themselves) put crochet, tatting, macramé, netting and knitting to every conceivable use. These techniques generally relied on cotton, although other fibres such as wool were used, especially in anything knitted for warmth. It is telling, however, that linen did not dominate this trend. Of its former significance only the term 'thread' remained, which until the early 1900s, and later in some regions, meant linen thread specifically: cotton threads were called 'cottons' to distinguish between the two.

The substitution of cotton for linen, while in part due to cotton's novelty and availability, also came about because of the difficulty of mechanizing linen spinning and weaving. Less elastic than cotton, hemp and flax snapped under the tension of early machine spinning, and it was only in about 1850 that wet

161, 162. European and North American linen-weaving traditions are represented here by two coverlets, one a linen–wool cloth with supplementary dyed woollen wefts, woven on a multi-heddle loom in about 1810 in Småland, Sweden (left), and the other woven in undyed linen and blue-dyed wool in Lafayette, Indiana and dated 1825. These patterns can also be compared to the carpets seen in ills 155, 163.

spinning, first attempted during the 1820s, was sufficiently successful to warrant the introduction of power-weaving for linen sheeting and shirting. Luxury linen handweaving survived, but many cloths formerly made with hand-spun linen warps were now made with machine-spun cotton ones. These include virtually all the former linen/cotton combinations such as denim and the fustians such as jean. The latter thus became an all-cotton cloth with less body than before, and it may be that this more flaccid handle contributed to the decline of English and American amateur crewelwork, in which loosely twisted brightly dyed worsted yarns had been embroidered onto white jean since its introduction in about 1560.

Many linen and silk, wool or worsted combinations disappeared with the rise of cotton, among them a favourite for whole-cloth quilts, linsey-woolsey. (Its linen warp denoted by Linsey, a 'new draperies' town in East Anglia: worsted – in this case the weft – was the region's speciality). Linen also disappeared from coverlets handwoven in bold designs playing a white warp against a dyed woollen weft. Known in North America as 'over-shot', 'summer and winter' and 'double weave', their making was indebted to Dutch, English, German, Scandinavian and Scottish

163. Amid the luxuries in this Berlin royal interior of 1824–40, are numerous examples of the 'hidden' uses of flax and hemp: under-upholstery cloths, the ground of the pile carpet, and the 'tent' on which the upholstery and cushions were embroidered, appropriately, in 'Berlin work' (named after the source of printed charts for worsted counted-thread work, issued from 1804).

immigrants, who originally also wove all-linen cloths. By the 1830s – when costly Jacquard-woven versions became available in eastern regions – only remote areas still provided itinerant weavers with home-spun linen yarns. More typically, until their weaving declined in the 1870s, it was only the patterns that represented these vanishing linen-weaving traditions.

Linen went behind the scenes. By the 1830s it was recommended for lining 'working gowns' (of printed cottons) because unlike the latter, it did not shrink when washed and so helped to

164. The roller-printed cotton samples in a book of 1806–17 from Jonathan Peel's Church Bank printworks in Lancashire, England, include numerous examples of discharge printing, particularly apparent where small white motifs occur on black or red grounds.

retain the garment's shape. Likewise, silk, merino and woollen bodices were lined with the same, to prevent these showier fabrics (made of far more elastic fibres) from stretching while being worn. For the same reasons flax and hemp – and, by the 1830s, jute – were common for flat-woven carpet warps, as entire grounds in pile carpets, and as backings in linoleum (introduced in 1861). All bore the same 'linen' patterns as the coverlets made in North America. Tent, the old term for linens used in counted-thread techniques – hence the terms 'tent stitch' for *petit point* and 'tent' for an embroidery frame – remained in use only when concealed with thick and quickly stitched worsted 'Berlin work' into which chenille, silk threads and beads were sometimes worked. For sewing, 'thread' was much more durable than 'cotton': the former was thus needed in bookbinding or on linen cloths or leather, waxed for additional strength when the work was heavy, as it was in countryman's smocks, aprons, and other utilitarian outerwear. Cotton encroached even here, in the form of light canvas (named from *cannabis*, so originally 'hemp').

Only the deeply ingrained appreciation of the longevity and subtle beauty of plain, sturdy hemp and flax cloths, as witnessed in late 19th-century China, provided any form of resistance to

the rise of machine-spun cotton. Occasionally, these and other hardy fibre-bearing plants were incorporated into the numerous projects initiated between the 1840s and the 1930s to introduce (or reintroduce) textiles into rural economies in order to moderate the iniquitous results of industrialization and colonization. An early example was the introduction in around 1825 to the Portuguese Azores of the century plant, *Agave americana*: its aloe fibre became the basis for a delicate knitting, called 'Azores lace'. Nevertheless, although the majority of such endeavours were based on constructions well suited to bast fibres – such as rug weaving, quilting and lacemaking – cotton was far more commonly used. In the West, the conscious revival of bast-fibre cloths was confined to followers of the late 19th- and early 20th-century Arts and Crafts movements, who preferred the natural shades of these fibres. Such initiatives, and the ease of growing hemp, preserved bast fibre crops, which are today grown in Russia, India and elsewhere, although the European crops are used mainly in paper-making.

Whiteness was also part of the issue. With the introduction of powdered chlorine and lime bleach in about 1800, the time required for bleaching cottons shortened to days, but for linen it was reduced only to weeks, as it still had to be crofted (laid out, or 'grassed'). This more effective bleach had important consequences for dyed patterns too. Discharge prints on cotton quickly became feasible at a reasonable price and were often extremely delicate. The 'lapis style' incorporated a mordant with the bleaching paste, so making a perfect exchange of one colour for another: a red madder dot on a discharged indigo ground, for example. A bleached cloth lent brilliance and clarity to dry- and immersion-dyed colours, and it was so important for mordant dyes and for discharging Turkey red that until the 1950s the most effective formula was called 'madder bleach'. The old caustic soda solution was now used for different purposes. Mercerization, patented by John Mercer in 1844 (but not refined to its present formula until the 1890s), treats cotton yarns and cloths under tension with this alkali, followed by a neutralizing acid bath. As a result, the fibres swell permanently, becoming more receptive to dyes and more lustrous.

By the mid-19th century, Britain was the leading supplier of good-quality dyed and printed cotton cloths and yarns to markets around the world (some of which it continued to dominate until the 1950s). The huge-flowered white and indigo or white and scarlet *pareo* cloths of the South Sea Islands, for example,

165. Despite its name, Azores lace is knitted. Like antimacassars and the use of doilies as decorative mats, it was a 19th-century innovation. Unusually, however, it was worked not in cotton but in aloe-fibre yarns.

16

166. By 1900–20, when this embroidered appliqué wall-hanging was made in northern Bihar, India, its all-cotton content was unlikely to have been manufactured locally. Instead, the machine-woven cloth undoubtedly came from Britain, while the threads had several possible European sources, important among them DMC (Dollfus-Mieg & Compagnie), a long-established firm on the French–German border still famous for its cotton threads and its association with the 19th-century embroiderer, Thérèse de Dillmont.

were designed and made in the Manchester region. After about 1850, cottons were exported from the United States, many to Latin America. Competition to obtain and to produce cottons became severe during the American Civil War, and the resulting 'cotton famine' of the 1860s had worldwide consequences. So, too, did the development of railways: goods moved quickly but tracks bypassed rural producers, thus hastening the dominance of machine-made goods and, especially on the Indian sub-continent and in central Asia, reducing their handweaving and block-printing to near extinction. The former area became a net importer of British textiles, while the latter became dependent on Russian textiles. Both were reduced to producing raw cotton for the manufacturing countries. It was a period of crisis and emigration. The decline began in Indian hand spinning, which had been sustained by internal markets and the continued external appreciation of the greater quality and durability of cotton cloths made from hand-spun yarns. Only craft-scale production survived beyond the 1920s. Similar pictures

can be painted for indigenous hand-production everywhere. Nevertheless, Indian weavers survived by making coarser cotton and bast-fibre goods, and productivity increased from 1867. In 1950, there still remained over three million handlooms in India and Pakistan.

In the complex dynamics of the shift from linen to cotton, the latter became the cloth of the people. However, two possibly unexpected things happened. One was in relation to marketing strategies: cottons wore out and so, perhaps, became the first manufactured goods with inbuilt obsolescence. The other concerned consumption and the response to the physical and aesthetic limitations of cottons. Except for cloths such as *pareo*, batiks for West Africa, or other culture-specific prints, many more bore very small all-over designs (the forte of machine printers), were plain dyed, or were bleached brilliant white. Both the relatively low resistance to wear and 'plainness' of cottons therefore contributed to vivid and varied uses of appliqué, patchwork and quilting around the world. Quilting, in particular, lent

167. Since the 19th century, the Kuna Indian women of the San Blas islands (off the Caribbean coast of Panama) have composed colourful *molas* entirely from plain-dyed machine-woven cotton cloth. A similar type of reverse appliqué is made by the White H'mong of Laos.

great strength to the completed work. The anonymity of mass-produced cotton cloths and yarns was nullified by these creative interventions, which remained characterized by home production, whether San Blas *molas*, Rajasthani *ralli*, Indo-Chinese reverse appliqué (as the previous two also are), Egyptian appliqué tent hangings, or the distinctly different patchwork quilts of Bangladesh (*kantha*) and North America.

For the industry, the shortage of cotton in the 1860s induced more creative thinking, resulting in more yarns spun from wastes, new varieties of mixed-fibre cloths and more intensive attempts to make 'artificial' yarns. Of these attempts, the most successful established the viscose process, based on an English patent of 1892. Viscose (rayon) combined cellulose from wood pulp or cotton linters, caustic soda and acid – that familiar list of ingredients – and was available in commercial quantities by the early 1900s for making cellophane. By the 1920s and 1930s, the viscose process provided a range of fibres tailormade for diverse products, from clothing to the reinforcing cords inside tyres. Although for a time called 'art silk' and chemically identical to cotton, the sheen, superior strength and variety of end uses of viscose were more typical of bast fibres. In addition, by 1950 viscose was significantly cheaper than cotton. In an ironic turn of events, cotton's reign was to be ended by a regenerated fibre in many ways like flax and hemp.

Chapter 9:   New Technology 1600–2000

An explanation of the assigned patents for textile machinery or recipes for new dyes and fibres since 1600 would itself fill several volumes. So too would a discussion of the many developments that were never patented, since these fixed-term monopolies (still a new concept in 1600) were intended only for inventions differing substantially from existing technologies. Both categories included minor amendments, false starts or short-lived finds, overtaken by other processes. Some concepts lay dormant until other advances made their use relevant. Their dates and inventors have in a few cases become legendary, but the truth is that most inventions – even the best known among them – were the result of long periods of refinement by many people and were often only applied to any extent twenty or thirty years later (especially if a patent restricted distribution). In addition, their dispersal typically resulted from further modifications. As a result, decades passed while new concepts filtered through regions or specializations. However, if accepted widely, the character of textile production changed, and old regional associations with particular fibres or technologies were altered.

As already indicated, the introduction of machine spinning resulted in a transformation of the cotton industries. Its impact on the social, economic and political balance around the world was accompanied by a modification of qualitative expectations and the eventual inclusion of even the most isolated of peoples in its consumption as yarn, cloth or ready-made clothing. Silk, in contrast, remained an exclusive fibre. Nevertheless, its high status – and thus potentially higher profit margins – propelled many key technical and organizational developments that presaged those adopted by the cotton industry. As was the case for cottons (and all cloths), the location of key silk-weaving centres was determined by the ability to create a sufficiently strong warp thread. So, in 1600 European production was either concentrated in Italy or dependent upon Italian – or more distant – supplies of organzine (as the fine hard-twisted silk for warps is called). Italy remained the source of technical innovation in silk processing and weaving for another century. Its mechanisms for silk yarn production were published in 1607 by Zonca in *Novo Teatro di Machine* but, despite subsequent editions in 1620 and 1686, its diffusion was largely dependent upon first-hand experience.

168. Many recent advances in textile technology have resulted from scientific and military necessity. The most demanding end-uses are epitomized by spacesuits. Recent examples begin with a sewn-tube and water-cooled garment over which lie nylon and fabric ventilation ducts. The outer suit might have sixteen layers made of Neoprene-coated nylon, aluminized Mylar layered with a non-woven polyester, Kapton for thermal protection and, outermost, two layers of flame-resistant cloth woven in Teflon-coated filaments.

169. The globalization of textile production made this 19th-century handwoven Guatemalan *huipil* possible. Its ground is cotton, once a luxury fibre in Latin America, while the finger-woven pattern is of silk, little used in the Americas until the 18th-century dispersal of silk-throwing technology.

170. The viability of this ciselé velvet depends on the strong organzine warps (the verticals) which in 1600 Italy alone in Europe could make. The same country was also an important source of metal threads formed by wrapping a silk core, as seen in the continuous weft loops.

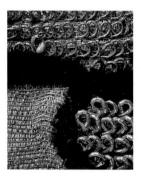

For example, when in 1718 Thomas Lombe established water-powered throwing machines in his Derby factory (the first of any kind in Britain), the machines were supervised by Italian workmen brought from Piedmont by Lombe's brother, John.

Silk cloth was undoubtedly the first to be printed by intaglio methods. The engraving of copper plates for printing on paper had evolved in Germany and Italy between 1425 and 1450, and etching with acids – using a needle to draw through a wax resist – appeared soon after 1500, developed from a method of decorating weapons and armour. Later methods, mezzotint and aquatint, work by removing engraved textural grounds (in concept, like discharging) and resisting acid with a sprinkled resin, respectively. The little-explored links between paper printing and textile printing begin with parallel functions – to carry imagery and information – and extend to printed guidelines for embroidery (on cloth), grids for weave-diagrams (on paper), and promissory notes. From the latter came bank notes, today viewed as a replacement for coinage, but of printed cellulose and

171. Intaglio printing methods carry the colourant in incised depressions rather than on the surface (as in block-printing). This silk handkerchief, copper-plate-printed by J. Cluer in London between 1667 and 1727, employs images after Wenceslas Hollar (1607–77), the Prague-born, Frankfurt-trained engraver and watercolourist who settled in London soon after 1636.

172. Significant German developments in printing on paper made this region an important source of textile printing expertise. Here, a block-printed linen of 1675–1700 demonstrates the skill of the block-cutter and, in its lace-like pattern, the wider influences of German pattern-books.

thus, in a sense, a modern form of 'cloth as currency'. The two main types of printing presses are essentially variations on screw-type linen presses or mangles which draw cloth between closely set rollers. The latter, compressing the plate and dampened cloth together, was the type used to print silks and a method that, given Italy's lead in European silk processing, possibly originated there. Early examples of silk printed in this fashion have survived from Germanic regions (since medieval times important producers of cold block-prints, often stamped in gold or silver in imitation of Byzantine and Italian silks). By the 1600s, rolling-presses were certainly printing silks in London, where oral tradition has it that all calico printers were originally silk printers. The critical difference is that whereas *lengths* of cotton or 'union' (linen and cotton) cloths were being block-printed with Indian-type mordant dyes in London and several continental European centres by the late 17th century, only large squares of plate-printed silks survive from the same period. Until the early 1800s, many were over-embroidered.

The key to successful block-printing for immersion or cold dyeing was the thickening of the colourant with a gum so that it adhered to the block for transfer to the cloth. Such viscous substances were well-known to paper printers, as were dye-matter inks. Although a direct connection between those who plate-printed silks and those who plate-printed lengths of plant fibre cloths has yet to be confirmed, it does appear that the William Sherwin who patented mordant block-printing in London in 1676 was the same William Sherwin who plate-printed silks there. Furthermore, the few surviving plate-printed wallpapers of the late 17th century bear a remarkable resemblance to the designs and repeats of plate-printed linen, cotton and union cloths, first documented as printed by Francis Nixon in Ireland in 1752 and brought to the outskirts of London four years later. Such precedents, together with the complex cross-selvedge repeats of mid-18th-century examples, indicate that it was by then a well-practised craft rather than an entirely new one. It was additionally established in Switzerland and a few French towns, including Sèvres, when, in 1770, Oberkampf adopted this technique for what in English is called *toile de Jouy*. (That the French called the same technique *toile d'Irelande* acknowledges their source, although expertise for this and other hand-printing

173. The first Jouy design commissioned from Jean-Baptiste Huet (1745–1811) celebrated Oberkampf's receipt of royal support for his Jouy-en-Josas factory in 1783–84. Copper-plate-printed on imported Indian cotton, it illustrates aspects of printing including, from top, 'grassing' (laying out cloth in order to bleach it), block-printing, and plate-printing itself.

174. A pantograph operator traces a design which is then engraved onto the roller in a repeating sequence. This concept (based on the 'mill and dye' technique invented in 1808) was first seen in the Swiss 'hand-machine' controls for double-eyed embroidery needles, which had been perfected by 1828. Pantographs survive in today's Shifflis and are widely used in mould-engraving and related applications.

methods more often came from England, Germany, Holland, Scotland and Switzerland.) Plate-printing, which also occurred in North America and, possibly, India, was gradually superseded by roller-printing but remained in use for another century, especially for printing commemorative items, particularly on silk.

By 1783–85 mechanized roller-printing, credited to Joseph Bell, was in use in Lancashire, England. At the same time, machine-printing was recorded in Colmar and Wesserling (both today in eastern France). Many early rollers may well have been made of wood inserted with metal pins, as was already done to add details to wooden printing blocks. Initially limited, like flat-plate-printing, to one colour with additional colours added by block or hand, by 1815 numerous improvements and variations emerged that allowed two-colour printing. These improvements included engraved copper rollers, machines combining copper rollers with wooden (surface) rollers, and a mechanized form of printing with discontinuous blocks (perrotine). Important among other innovations was the introduction of 'mill and dye' engraving by Joseph Lockett of Manchester in about 1808, which also marked a significant advance in banknote printing. In this technique, a relief-patterned steel cylinder, run several times around a copper roller, impressed in days the complex small patterns formerly taking several months by hand. Lockett's, considered to be Britain's foremost textile engraving firm, implemented other improvements and had global influence. In the following twenty years the means of engraving rollers was refined and a third colour roller introduced.

The parallels between paper, wallpaper and textile presses remained pertinent, and much of their imagery was shared. While methods such as lithography were tried out on cloth (again, particularly on silk), between the 1840s and the 1950s textile printing was dominated by ever-faster and more complex

175. Printed sheets and towels were an innovation of the 1960s supported by the development of screen-printing machines up to 3 metres (10 feet) wide, resin-bonded pigments, and more advanced photo-engraving techniques. An ironic response to the explosion of consumption, *Restless Sleeper/Atomic Shroud*, by the American artist Robert Morris (b. 1931) was hand-screen-printed in 1981 at the Fabric Workshop (founded in Philadelphia in 1977).

176. In 1910, the Spanish-born Mariano Fortuny y Madrazo (1871–1949, active in Venice from 1889) patented a continuous stencil-printing machine with a silk mesh and photographically produced barrier. This silk velvet long gown of 1929–30 was stencilled with metallic pigment.

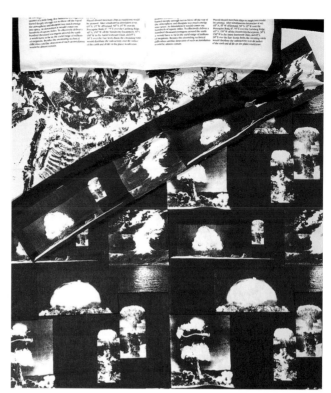

engraved copper-roller printing machines. Hand block-printing – initially boosted by its use on one-colour machine-printed cloths – remained fairly widespread until the Second World War and remains a specialist craft today. Block-printing was particularly important for printing textured and high-quality cloths, and was only really threatened with the arrival of hand screen-printing in the 20th century.

The reopening of Japan to the outside world in the 1860s may have induced greater interest in the artistic possibilities of stencil printing and probably influenced Pacific Islanders, who adopted tapa stencilling in this period. Nevertheless, a related technique – screen-printing – represents the convergence of established Western stencilling techniques with two other developments: the isolation of more synthetic dyes from the 1870s onwards and inventions in the 1870s and 1880s aimed at stenographers, signmakers and product labellers. The inventions included patents by A. B. Dick and David Gestetner, who in the United States and Britain respectively founded the duplicating-machine companies bearing their names (Dick also used patents by Thomas Edison). The closest forebear of the textile handscreen – today a frame stretched with sheer cloth (originally silk) and supporting a block-out substance – was patented in 1887 in the United States by Charles Nelson Jones of Michigan, in the heart of American grain land. Flour sacks appear to have been its first sustained textile application. Of subsequent developments little is currently clear, except that the Dutch contributed their long-established blowing technique, and between 1894 and 1910 patents were lodged in several countries for spray-painting or dry-dyeing textiles, with hand-positioned screens or with continuous stencils. Large-scale printing of American flags from 1915, using a British patent of 1907, confirmed the technique's commercial viability; soon afterwards several other patents improved image-making and colour-delivery systems, the latter including the squeegee. Far less expensive than block-making, screens finally came into their own for hand-printing in the 1930s; semi-automatic and fully automatic machines were widespread by the 1950s. By the 1970s rotary screen-printing and another 'interdisciplinary' technique – called 'offset', 'transfer' or 'sublistatic' printing and akin to methods for both ceramics and paper – were the only forms of printing or weaving cloth that continued to expand significantly in terms of volume of production.

Machine knitting differs substantially from weaving and printing and it was the fastest growing industry in the 20th century, over which time it became highly fashionable and was used worldwide. It is estimated that one in five garments worn today is knitted. In addition, the development of knitting has been responsible for the most striking and fundamental changes in textiles and clothing since 1600. Its complex history can be charted in some detail: the invention by William Lee in 1589 of a hand-operated frame for knitting coarse woollen stockings; his initial disappointment at its reception in London and rapid adaptation for silk; his second failure to obtain a patent in England and removal to Rouen and then Paris in the early 1600s; and on his death, his brother James's return. By the 1620s, James and a former Lee apprentice (who had meanwhile improved the frame) were established in Nottinghamshire in the English Midlands, the area that would subsequently dominate the production of hosiery in worsted and, after 1730, Indian and then British cotton. London frame knitters specialized in silk. Although attempts were also made to create silk frame-knitting cottage industries in Italy and Holland, it was not until much later that

177. *Hands*, 2000, were machine-knitted in grillon nylon, heat formed and metallized by Frances Geeson, who in the 1990s discovered that such conductive fibres could be used as switching devices. Collaborations with companies such as Philips Research developed interactive fabrics for wearable computer applications and other related uses.

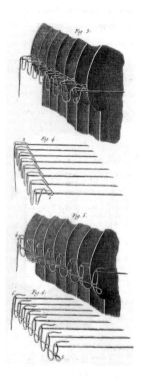

the Midlands had any serious rivals. Among the frame's key components were barbed needles, one for each loop, into which hand operated 'fingers' simultaneously pushed a pass of continuous yarn while removing the previous pass to create a row of loops. In all cases the resulting cloth was flat, and shaped (or 'fashioned') as it was made.

By about 1700 simple voided patterns were made by moving loops to adjacent needles, and from the mid-18th century, more fanciful designs appeared in white cotton hosiery (a term that came to include garments other than stockings). Numerous patents, improvements and off-shoots followed over the next 150 years. By then powered machines were being introduced, both flat and, for coarser and cheaper work, circular. A more automatic latched needle was developed in Britain in 1847, and this and the circular (or weft-knitting) machine were favoured in North America and Germany. For finer fashioned garments, Britain retained its original approach, industrializing only slowly, primarily with rotary-driven flat frames designed to knit several pieces simultaneously known as (William) Cotton's Patent type, introduced in 1864 and modified thereafter. This gradually eliminated the long-established practice of frame-renting to thousands of outworkers, whose circumstances had become desperate during the 19th century.

The stocking frame had four striking features. The first was the relatively early creation of the frame technique, given that substantial hand-knitting cottage industries in Spain and Italy (the European leaders in silk hand-knitting), and the United Kingdom and Swiss–German provinces (with worsteds), had emerged only during the 15th and 16th centuries. Lee was undoubtedly spurred on by the craze of his day for hand-knitted silk stockings from Spain or Italy, so costly that most still wore cut-cloth hose. The frame was thus arguably the first machine developed in response to specific consumer demands, and it certainly made the first shaped ready-made clothing. The second was the slow initial progress of its diffusion. While the countries above – and later Germantown, Philadelphia – had become important centres of hand frame-knitting by the 19th century, needle-knitting continued to flourish. In Scotland, for example, hand knitting provided significant employment in the Highlands well into the 20th century, while frame knitting, introduced during the 1680s, took another century to become a specialist industry of the lowland Borders region. Towns such as Hawick were entirely dependent for much of the 19th and 20th

178. The basic actions of a hand-operated stocking frame are the positioning of looped yarn through barbed needles (Fig. 3) and the closure of the barb to catch the next pass of the yarn (Fig. 4), which is then pushed over the barbs (Fig. 5) to create a knitted row (Fig. 6). This row is then pulled back and dropped over a new pass of yarn as the sequence is repeated.

179. These 18th-century women's silk stockings were made on a Lee and Paget or derivative stocking frame, possibly in Spain. Shaped as they were knitted and seamed afterwards, the decorative 'clocks' were inlaid as the knitting progressed.

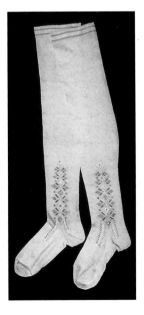

centuries upon the processing of soft fibres such as lambs-wool and cashmere. The explanation lay in part in the third feature, the discovery of a method of replicating needle and single-thread techniques (though until the introduction of machine power this was a laborious process). Knitting frames required specialist metal-smithing and marked the move away from carpentry, the basis of looms and embroidery frames, towards machine-building as an independent section of the textile industry. This required considerable capital, as did the patenting process and creation of small factories, which pre-dated powered technologies in knitting, as in many other textile processes.

The fourth and most noteworthy feature of the stocking frame was that it spawned a complex range of technologies. Its concepts of adapted needles, machine-assisted looping and voided patterns led to a variety of machine-made silk nets, for which there were dozens of British patents and improvements after 1750. Among these were 'Frost's net' of 1769 (which created plain stocking stitch on a mesh ground, patterned via a cylinder inserted with pins like a later printing roller or barrel organ); the 1771 improvements that refined the side-to-side motion of the needles; and the development in 1775 of warp knitting. The latter drew and secured loops sideways from the warp and was the first multi-thread knitting machine, giving a unique cloth construction used initially for solid coarse woollens and, from 1795, silk nets. Such principles provided paradigms, even direct inspirations, for other cloths. Finer warp-knitted jersey (plain) and tricot (ribbed) fabrics were being made by about 1800. From 1808 the runaway success was John Heathcoat's multi-thread bobbinet machine, with its twisting and traversed warp replicating hand bobbin-made droschel (a sexagonal mesh). Bobbinet was widely used until the 1830s as the basis for hand needle-run, appliquéd and tamboured nets. This and lacy warp knitting gave rise to a further frenzy of developments, including multi-thread machine-laces such as Pusher, Leavers and 'curtain' (or Nottingham), the latter an 1840s latecomer. Heathcoat's own machines, between 1818 and his death in 1860, were in operation in both England (water powered) and France (steam powered). The proof that a machine could duplicate the work of hand-held needles launched a raft of new developments: the Swiss pantograph-controlled, single-thread running-stitch 'hand-machine' for embroidery (1828), the American and British running-stitch and improved two-thread lock-stitch sewing machines (late 1840s, refined 1856–77), the related single-

185

174

180. The Scottish machine-lace industry was well established by the 1880s, when it also became a leader in the production of coordinated furnishing fabrics and – on both 'Nottingham' and leno gauze ('Madras') Jacquard looms – semi-sheer panels for windows. An 1899 design for the latter, by Hugh Maclachlan for Alexander Morton & Company, illustrates the type of boldly bordered patterns equally suited to hand-knotted rugs (which the company had begun producing in Ireland a year earlier).

181. Macclesfield became England's foremost silk town after the decline of Spitalfields, London, in about 1800. Among the products for which it became known were scarf, tie and cravat silks, often (as in this example from the 1850s) with details highlighted in brocading (or 'chintzing') by the use of swivelling loom-controlled bobbins.

thread chain-stitch Cornely embroidery machine (an 1870s improvement on the Bonnaz, patented 1863, using tambour hooks), and the two-thread lock-stitch powered Shiffli (successor to the hand-machine in the 1880s). All of these owed something to early knitting frames, as did several devices for looms.

Numerous knitting frame-related adaptations were made to handlooms during the 16th to 18th centuries, particularly those for small wares such as ribbons, chenille yarns, braids, garters and tapes that as a consequence became important aspects of interiors and fashions. During the 17th century, dozens of small wares began to be handmade at a time on what were called 'Dutch engines' or 'engine looms' – names serving as a reminder that 'engine' did not in this or the following century mean a mechanically powered device. In the late 1600s, improvements to the Dutch engine resulted in a new name, the 'swivel loom'. This produced finer products and in the 18th century incorporated localized bobbins, which moved side-to-side in order to insert numerous identical supplementary wefts. Its counterpart, the tappet loom, inserted localized supplementary warps. Both swivel and tappet looms were also used to make small patterns on loom-width cloths and remained in use into the 20th century for specialist products such as silk tie-cloths made in Macclesfield, England, and the muslins with little dot and geometric motifs for which Switzerland was famous.

For large-scale patterns the most significant development was an improvement to the drawloom exhibited in Paris in 1801 by Joseph-Marie Jacquard and taking his name. It was intended for, and was first used by, the silk industry in France, but was only really embraced by weavers once it was adapted for larger patterns. The technology was acquired by stealth for English manufacture in 1820 and was soon known elsewhere on the continent and in North America. In evolved form it replaced the weaver's assistant with two overhead series of joined punched cards. The larger set reversed and made more flexible the barrel-organ principle by allowing or halting the rise of metal rods – significantly, often called 'needles' – which in turn controlled the warp threads for patterning. The other set of cards created the ground weave. One foot treadle alone was needed and this eased its transition to powered weaving; connected by a cord to an overhead ratchet, each depression positioned the next card, one for each passage of weft. Even when worked by hand it was considerably faster than the drawloom, especially when combined with the fly shuttle developed by John Kay in England in 1733 (but not much used until the later 18th century). However, the drawloom fell from use only slowly. In the 1920s one was still being used to train apprentices in the Warner & Sons silk mill in Essex, England; other firms across Europe did the same, and their limited use continues today in France, Italy and Spain.

182. A Jacquard mechanism sits above a five-frame hand-operated Brussels carpet loom, with its large pattern-controlling series of cards on the right. The frames are typical of all warp-pile looms and provide the supply of the warps to be looped, while the ground warp is supplied under tension from below.

[Brussels-Carpet Loom.]

From about 1820 to 1860, the Jacquard became commonly and widely used for most kinds of Western handwoven luxury goods such as laces and cashmere shawls. (Its progress elsewhere is not well documented.) Its impact was apparent in two particular ways. The first was in the profusion of realistic imagery, which exploited the ability to control each warp thread. The second was in the transformation of carpets into a much more affordable commodity. Between 1825 and 1830, the Jacquard was refined for pileless and moquette looms, as well as the British equivalents of the latter, Wilton and Brussels. Powered versions followed in the 1840s, patented in both the United States and the United Kingdom by Erastus Brigham Bigelow of Lowell, Massachusetts. In the same decade cross-fertilization between carpet, coverlet and cloth weaving resulted in many new variations of pile weaves, as well as power-woven tapestry (soft, weft-intensive fabrics similar in construction, and sometimes in pattern, to Jacquard-woven shawls). For the first time the expanding middle classes had an abundance of velvets, moquettes, plushes and richly figured cloths and lace fabrics, for both interiors and clothing.

From the 1860s to 1880s, Jacquard power-machines making fair imitations of hand-knotted carpets (and hence called 'Axminsters') were developed in the United States and improved

183. Printing and weaving were combined to create very affordable ikat-velvet-like 'Tapestry Brussels' carpet, its looped-pile pattern created by pre-printing the wool warps (the ground is jute and linen). In wide use by the late 1840s, the printing drum was patented in Scotland in 1832 and replaced a fifty-year-old French block-printing method. This Japanese-influenced pattern of about 1880 was made by Roxbury Carpet Company in Boston, Massachusetts, the centre of industrial textile production in the United States until the 1920s.

184. Pre-patterned yarns could be made by weaving variously coloured wefts across grouped warps. When the completed cloth was slit between each group, the warps were twisted to form a chenille yarn. Their use was extended to carpets from about 1840 and to tablecovers and curtains soon afterwards. Richly patterned and coloured cotton chenille table covers, such as this North American example, became more widely available, and by 1900 could be acquired quite cheaply.

in Britain. By 1895, Jacquards were applied to the last of the major 19th-century machines, the Shiffli. Further improvements in the early 1900s made power-driven Jacquards faster, and speed remained the focus in all areas of textile technology until about 1970. A similar scenario can be sketched out for the vast array of looms for smaller patterns with cam, barrel-and-peg and punched-card or -tape controls – broadly classed as 'dobby looms' – which became more specialized and productive. By 1970 air-jet and water-jet weft insertion had made weaving the same cloth fifteen times faster than in 1900 (and over three hundred times faster than in the mid-18th century.) Despite mid-20th-century standardization, so many different loom types were developed that even those dedicated to making plain-weave cloths still have hundreds of variations to accommodate specific yarns, loom widths and environmental conditions. Computer-controlled patterning, which took off in the 1980s – led by the knitting sector – was the logical next step, given that computer data was originally input via miniature versions of the Jacquard's punched cards. It counteracted standardization by almost eliminating the down time formerly required to change patterns, and became a significant feature in

both design development and, during the 1990s, an aspect of sampling (the high-cost element of textile production).

Machine knitting also supported the development of yarns, and British cotton spinning was especially closely intertwined with this industry. For example, in 1835 the perfection of a fine two-ply cotton yarn for net machines aided the further development of lace machines. During the 20th century this symbiotic relationship transferred to the regenerated cellulose fibres, viscose and acetate, and to the synthetic fibres derived from petrochemical feedstocks. All were initially difficult to print and, in some cases, to dye, but were suited to knitting. The first of the synthetics was nylon, which took nearly twelve years to develop, had wool-like characteristics, and was available in the United States in late 1939. Polyester was available in 1946, followed quickly by the acrylics. Since then these have been modified many times over for better handling and specialized end-uses, from the industrial to the ephemeral. By the 1950s, synthetics manufacturers had taken over from dye companies as the leading applied organic chemists and promoted not only new fibres but also new dyes and the wider application of warp knitting – for example, in upholstery – as well as the development of 'non-wovens' and related products such as tufted carpets. These multifaceted needle-punched, bonded, heat-set, laminated or abraded textiles range from the everyday, such as hospital gowns and cleaning cloths, to high performance architectural, aeronautical, geophysical, industrial, military and medical materials.

The appetite for stretch whetted by knitwear was also fed by the perfection of synthetic rubber (elastane/spandex) filaments, which must be spun with another fibre to make a viable yarn or woven with a stable yarn to create a stretch fabric. The best known among these, Lycra, has been available since 1958. During the 1970s new spinning technology was developed in Japan, giving micro-fibres far finer than human hair. Natural fibre production could no longer keep pace with the increasing world population, and by the mid-1980s only about one-quarter of fibres consumed were cotton. Since the full spectrum of demands now had to be met by regenerated and synthetic fibres, thousands of 'techno textiles' arose. Discussed frequently in issues of *Textile Horizons* – published for The Textile Institute, which from its base in Manchester, England, represents the industry worldwide – by 2000 new technological breakthroughs included the genetic engineering of wool and advanced laser-printing techniques. The pace quickened, but such innovation

185. The most successful initial application of regenerated and synthetic yarns has generally been in knitted items, such as this warp-knitted (Raschel) shawl of the 1920s or 1930s. Identical patterns in blended polyester-cotton yarns were again fashionable in the 1970s and, in further modified yarns, around 2000. Its vertical wavy bands exploit the side-to-side motion inherent in warp knitting.

186. Spinners have made a substantial contribution to both innovative design and cloth behaviour. In 18th-century Lyon (which, as a result of reorganization in the 1660s by the French minister Colbert, had become the centre for luxury French silks), many cloth structures were devised primarily to highlight the characteristics of new yarns such as chenille. Here, the alternating horizontal stripes are composed of four to seven picks of metal *lamella* (flat) and the same of *frisé* (crimped) – a technique called *brillant*.

was not itself new. Nor was it all based on new technology. The trial weavings for automobile nylon air bags were carried out on century-old Scottish 'madras' (leno) looms; the slings propelling space-launched satellites are warp-knitted; and the cloth formation with fire- and puncture-proof meta-aramid and stronger-than-steel Kevlar fibres (the latter, like Lycra, a DuPont registered trade name) is often a plain weave.

Despite the attention given to new fibres, one aspect of textile *design* seldom attracting study (except in medieval and earlier periods) is the composition and construction of yarns themselves. Alteration of texture, component elements and degree of twist can produce radical changes in the appearance and performance of cloths. Yarn and cloth finishing, except fulling and printing, also attracts little attention, although rubberizing, metallizing, waxing, oiling, plasticizing, hot

187. Calendering for smoothness and embossing of textures or patterns are among many long-used and little-studied finishing techniques. Both were employed on this 17th-century Indian twilled silk and silver-thread cloth with coloured brocading wefts.

'de-fuzzing', mercerization and other treatments to render surfaces smooth or impervious have long been important to the character and function of many textiles. Rubber itself was used for protective clothing from about 1830; metallizing dates from the same period. A cloth of smooth-spun yarn remains essential for detailed printing and was part of the appeal of Indian cottons to European copper-plate printers. The Indian skill in finishing was equally significant. Until the 1730s Gujarati weavers tailored their techniques to the tastes of their Middle Eastern buyers and in 1664 the English East India Company reported that cotton cloths intended for the markets of Persia, Basra and Mokha would not sell there unless they were starched and glazed as smooth as paper. It might be conjectured that the idea of press-printing on cotton began with the European importation of such cloths, but this – and the nature of the recipes for these and older finishes – has yet to be established.

Invention also directed the hand-making of textiles, as technique and design worked together. Although industrial textile journals were already by the 1830s referring to a 'global village', individual makers, even when grouped together by putting-out and factory systems, long combined intuitive discovery, reinvention of techniques known elsewhere, and ignorance of the 'how to' behind imported textiles. This phenomenon is well recorded from the 18th century onwards. For example, the French embroiderer St Aubin summarized in 1770 the characteristics of different nations' techniques. After giving praise to Dresden work ('the finest and most perfect') and Viennese embroiderers, citing the excessive cost of Milanese and Venetian embroideries, and noting the embroidered skins of Senegalese women, the snakeskin, fur and human-hair embroideries of Canada and the spiral gold wire, insect bodies, claws, fruit stones and feathers of the Indians, he then lingered over Chinese, Ottoman and Lyonnaise work. He judged the Chinese work with flat silk (floss), twisted silk and bark fibres to have unequalled precision and remarked that only they knew how to make yarns of gold paper wound around silk threads. (He was unaware that the Japanese also understood its making: a century later this 'Jap-gold' thread was introduced into Europe and quickly copied by the Germans.) Of Georgian and Turkish women working with the finest of gold thread he admitted that their delicate process was unknown in France. To Lyon he credited the use of paillettes and spangles, which certainly were fashionable until the 1820s but, as is now known, had ancient origins.

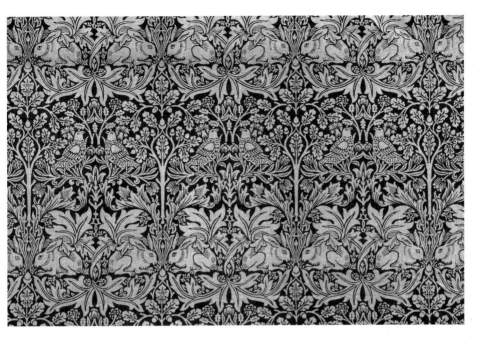

188. *Brer Rabbit* was designed by William Morris (1834–96) in 1882 and realized on cotton by block-printing a discharge on a deep blue indigo-dyed cloth. The bleaching is only partial, giving a light blue – an effect called 'semi-discharge'.

His compatriot Philippe de la Salle was closely involved in the silk industry of Lyon and he himself was rewarded for creating cloth constructions for which antecedents and independent descendants can be found elsewhere. In the next century in England William Morris 'revived' indigo, when in fact it was still in wide use. In the 1920s in the same country, Phyllis Barron and Dorothy Larcher 'discovered' lino block-printing. These examples serve as reminders of the discontinuity of knowledge which, advantageously, and even today, can spark new fashions and passions. They also indicate the level of secrecy or difficulty often surrounding successful techniques and hint at the way individuals, independently or within factories, constantly intervene with technological 'givens'.

Chapter 10:   The Art of Textiles 1850–Today

The art of textiles rests in contradiction. On the one hand the signals projected by textiles are determined by a particular selection from the never-ending possibilities offered by fibres, colours, constructions and patterns; on the other hand, their reception is tempered by every person's intimate – and often unconscious – knowledge of their textures, sounds, smells and appearance. The contradictions occur when this intuitive understanding (which generally overlooks the complexity of textiles) is confronted by a form or image that prompts a reconsideration of these assumptions. When only the richest wore and owned bright, intricately figured textiles, they easily commanded awe and projected prestige. While the further power-driven industrialization of textile processes between the 1820s and the 1860s did not debase tastes, as has often been claimed, it did render the personal experience of an array of decorative textiles more commonplace. Since that time only certain textiles have really been 'visible', becoming 'seen' by questioning accepted aesthetic concepts, challenging entrenched social attitudes, re-examining techniques, or being used in unexpected ways. While both makers and consumers have participated in such deliberate confrontations, their wider impact generally arose out of various forms of collective action, whether formal or informal in composition, and these are the focus of this chapter.

Many of these confrontations reflect the issues raised by successive well-known movements in Western art, craft and design. (The shifting connotations of these words are an interesting but separate subject. Here they represent the traditional boundaries created by price, audience, media and end-use.) Britain, with its powerful textile industry and the world's richest consumer market in the mid-19th century, provided the first of these: the Arts and Crafts movement. It was named after the Arts and Crafts Exhibition Society, initiated in 1887 in opposition to the annual exhibitions of London's Royal Academy (which had come almost exclusively to contain easel-paintings and had ceased entirely to exhibit the work of architects). The movement's basic principle – that the fine and applied arts were equals – had been formulated mid-century by such disparate supporters of rationalism and authenticity as John Ruskin and A. W. N. Pugin. London's Great Exhibition of 1851 (the first

189. Ed Rossbach (born Chicago, 1914) is a consummate craftsman, and is now known worldwide both for his work and his post-Second World War publications. His thorough knowledge of traditional techniques and creative use of them is only hinted at in this detail of an ash splint basket of 1992.

190. The Japanese-influenced Aesthetic Movement both preceded and contributed to the styles associated with the Arts and Crafts movement. These silk tissues were designed in 1870–75 by Bruce Talbert (1838–81), a British architect who also designed furniture, carpets and wallpapers. They were handwoven on Jacquard looms by Daniel Walters & Sons, Essex, England.

of a series of international exhibitions showcasing manufactured goods) had galvanized the emerging debate about who ought to be initiating designs, which in turn propelled numerous architects into designing for what were then termed the 'manufacturing arts'. As a result, by the 1870s textile design was already a substantial aspect of the foremost British architectural practices, and was included in the work of the several guilds, businesses (such as Morris & Company, 1861–1940), and small enterprises and cooperatives created in response to the same issues. Most, however, designed patterned textiles to be manufactured by established firms, albeit often using hand techniques such as block-printing or hand-Jacquard weaving.

As much a social movement as one concerned with aesthetics, by the 1890s there were several distinct expressions of the Arts and Crafts ethos. A repudiation of the separation of design from making and an emphasis on the moral and spiritual values of handwork underpinned the guiding concept of 'noble simplicity'. This was exercised in the three textile crafts – weaving, spinning and dyeing – by individuals running workshops and, occasionally, firms. In the cloths that resulted from this ethos, fibres, dyes and texture were everything, and natural irregularities were celebrated. Pattern held little interest, except when expressive of yarn or constructional qualities, or made in response to the cloth through embroidery or appliqué. As the movement's influence spread, 'noble simplicity' gained notable proponents such as the American Gustav Stickley (whose mixed flax and jute yarn Craftsman Canvases of 1901–16 were machine-spun and -woven in Scotland by Donald Brothers), the Frenchman Paul Rodier, and several later weavers at the German Bauhaus (1919–33). In Britain, the progress of 'noble simplicity' in the three crafts was stimulated by Ethel Mairet through her publications and workshop, Gospels, from 1914 until her death in 1952. She trained native and continental 191 weavers and, as an ardent and successful advocate for cooperation between individuals and industry, was by about 1930 positioning one with the other to initiate design developments for both yarns and cloths, launching, most notably, the English career of Swiss-born Marianne Straub. Gospels also had strong links with several Scandinavian studio-workshops. With little 192 textile industrialization, these drew upon an uninterrupted craft tradition to develop their own emerging mass production. In the United States, the influence of Scandinavian weavers was most pronounced at Cranbrook Academy of Art from 1930 until the early 1960s, although ex-Bauhaus weavers, others from elsewhere in Europe, and a seemingly independent western American movement were all articulating the subtle beauty of woven cloth. Everywhere during the same period modernist interiors, furniture and couture exploited its rugged materiality.

Among those behind the Arts and Crafts Exhibition Society were many members of the Art Workers' Guild, founded in London in 1884 and soon absorbing two earlier influential groups. The same source, then and for decades thereafter, provided the majority of Principals and staff at the Central School of Arts and Crafts in London, which was founded in 1896. Its aim was to preserve dying crafts and at the same time find new applications for these skills. All staff were active practitioners, teaching only part-time. May Morris, the daughter of

191. The influence of Ethel Mairet (which extended even to Mahatma Gandhi) is here indicated by two vivid hand-dyed, -spun and -woven samples of the 1930s (the plaid particarly typical of her workshop). Both were woven by Marianne Straub (1909–94), whose own exploration of weave structures included the distorted-warp sample of about 1983, inspired by Peruvian techniques.

William Morris, established embroidery classes in 1898 and tapestry was later taught by staff from Morris & Company's Mortlake tapestry works. Luther Hooper, who developed the 'craftsman drawloom', was instrumental in the weaving department, and the prolific designer Lindsay Butterfield taught surface design. For printed textiles, however, the significant influences were the calligrapher Edward Johnston and his pupil Noel Rooke. The latter revived, and from 1909 taught, the 'white line' style of wood (and linoleum) engraving within the Central School's book production department. Although other London art students, such as Barron and Larcher, took up block-printing, until the 1940s Rooke was the sustained force behind the impact of autographic (as opposed to reprographic) engraving in northern Europe and the United States. Rooke used his graver as a pen, mark-making directly onto the block. Collaborations across departments and with manufacturers disseminated this approach, which transformed the imagery into one based on seemingly spontaneous gestural marks – a far cry from the patterns carefully painted out for commercial production whether by hand or machine. Having broken the mould, the freedom of the 'white line' approach was inherited by experimental screenprinters, who still often work directly on the screen.

192. Although her workshop is rightly described as Sweden's most significant producer of handwoven textiles well into the 20th century, Märta Måås-Fjetterstrom, who wove this tapestry between 1926 and 1936, is but one of a number of Scandinavians whose approach contributed to concepts of modernity in many aspects of interiors, including textiles.

193. Trained by Noel Rooke in the 1920s, Joyce Clissold's mastery of the 'white line' style is apparent in *Pam Flowers*, printed from lino-blocks she cut in about 1935. At the time Clissold (1905–82) hand-printed with synthetic dyes, employed some forty people and had two London shops, and thus embodied the entrepreneurial spirit of craft-based production around the globe.

194. The artists' workshops established by the Wiener Werkstätte in 1913 provided unlimited materials in exchange for the artistic rights to designs. Those of Dagobert Peche (1886–1923), a prolific multi-disciplinarian, include *Glacier Flower*, a stencil and block-printed silk of about 1913.

Both the Arts and Crafts movement and the Central School contributed to the development of entrepreneurial and interdisciplinary textile practices in studios, schools, workshops and the art-into-industry initiatives that were especially apparent in northern Europe up to about 1940. These included the Wiener Werkstätte (Vienna, 1903–32), the Werkbunds designing for machine production from 1907 in Germany (and later in Austria, Switzerland and Sweden, all branching into textiles in the 1920s), the Bauhaus, and numerous *Kunstgewerbeschulen* (artwork schools) such as the one in Zurich where Straub had initially trained. Each organization had its own regional and ideological character. The Wiener Werkstätte, for example, reflected the vitality of its pivotal position at the helm of the Secessionist movement, at the heart of modern psychology (Sigmund Freud) and as the centre of European café society. In its day, it was the most commercially successful model for other approaches to artist-designed textiles, such as the Parisian Maison Martine – Paul Poiret's firm, founded in 1912 for the making and sale of fabrics designed by Raoul Dufy and others – and England's own Omega (1913–19), masterminded by the Post-Impressionist painter and art critic, Roger Fry. In the United States, where the Werkstätte had New York shops, these undoubtedly planted the seeds of later collaborations between several American galleries and textile manufacturers. The motives behind these enterprises ranged from providing additional revenue for artists or national industries to promoting art movements themselves. Until the mid-1960s their impact was most obvious in printed fabrics, by which time the concept of artist-designed textiles was well established in all of these countries, as well as in Italy.

Such prints played a major role in International Style interiors and contributed to the increasingly blurred divisions between fine art and textiles. Such boundaries were at the same time being challenged by tapestry weavers. In a handful of ateliers an opposition to the reduction of the technique to an imitative art led to a rejection of fine weaving and an unlimited palette in favour of coarser yarns and a limited range of colours. In the years immediately following the Second World War, there were many artist-designed tapestries in circulation, and those by Dufy, Matisse, Miró, Picasso and others have since become well known. However, these did not generate change, and were not a new concept. Artist-designed tapestries had been woven in the interwar period elsewhere in Europe and in the United States,

195. Nathalie du Pasquier
(born France, 1957) gained an
international reputation for
her contribution to the Italian
interior and product design group.
Memphis. Based in Milan from
1981 to 1988, it promoted an
eclectic Post-Modernist mixture
of surface colours, patterns and
shapes, as manifested in *Gabon*.
a screen-printed cotton of 1982
inspired by the arts of Africa,
India and Australia.

and even these overshadow the many barely documented wall-hangings and rugs produced in numerous workshops in the same years. For the tapestry weavers of the 1950s, it was instead the raw, vivid imagery of the Aubusson tapestries designed by the French artist Jean Lurçat that had the greatest 'visibility'. 196 In terms of technique itself, Lurçat's influence is most evident in the work of Archie Brennan. The latter's design direction of the Edinburgh Tapestry Company between 1957 and 1977, his formation in 1962 of the tapestry department in that city's college of art, and his mid-1970s recommendations regarding the policy of the Victorian Tapestry Workshop led British and Australian weavers to interact more directly with imagery. By around 1990, an informal coalition encompassing these countries, as well as the Americas, had brought about the renaissance of tapestry. Work such as the unique 'overshot' tapestry technique of Swedish-born and -trained Helena Hernmarck (who emigrated to Canada in 1964, before moving to Connecticut) further fuelled the debate surrounding construction itself.

Although imagery is essential to tapestry weavers, during the 1960s and 1970s the questioning of technique coincided with the transformation of other constructed textiles. These paid greater attention to the sculptural, non-pictorial qualities inherent in textiles. Fibres and dyes remained core elements of expression, but often at a scale that placed the emphasis on form. The vibrant, gutsy 'waterfalls' of knotted sisal and cotton by the American Claire Zeisler epitomize this exploration of a

196. This detail of a 1945 Aubusson tapestry, designed by French artist Jean Lurçat (1892–1966), reveals the coarser weave and more limited colour palette that underpinned the subsequent resurgence of tapestry as an artistic medium.

towering and demanding presence. As the weaving industry contracted – eliminating opportunities for all but the most determined of handweaving cloth designers – such work seemed to say, 'fibres *will* be seen'. A minimum size of five square metres was introduced at Switzerland's Lausanne Biennale (1962–*c.* 1995). This became a crucial international forum particularly for those from the Far East and behind the 'Iron Curtain', such as Magdalena Abakanowicz, whose work said, '*we* will be seen'.

Not surprisingly, the 1970s saw a rebuttal of the idea that 'big was best' in the form of a series of biennial miniature international touring textile exhibitions (starting in England, then hosted by other countries, from Australia to Hungary). In the same decade the move away from 'noble simplicity' became most apparent in the highly controlled and impersonal gauzes of the English weaver, Peter Collingwood, who decried the mark of the maker. Everywhere work gradually became increasingly contemplative and conceptual. That it placed more demands on the viewer was an indication of the confidence fibre artists had gained in the space of a few decades. At the same time, textiles began to form key elements in installations and site works such

197. Made between 1976 and 1982, *Backs* by Polish-born Magdalena Abakanowicz were originally constructed from jute, burlap and resin. They were later cast in bronze and contributed both to the repositioning of fibre arts and to the increasing sensuality of minimalist art.

as Christo's *Running Fence* (1976). This incorporation of 'depersonalized' textiles only served to blur the boundaries further. Since then both technical and conceptual textiles have mainly explored questions of authentic versus counterfeit, animate versus inanimate, human versus mechanical, with such 'invisible' fabrics as blown synthetic sheets and loom-woven coated tarpaulins (typically used on trucks) becoming significant aspects of sculpture and architecture.

198

In defining and validating the art of textiles, many different roles have been played by museums, which in their current form originated in the mid-19th century. Private collections and public processions had for centuries been the primary forms of textile display, but relied on the discretion of owners. This changed as a result of the celebratory and competitive nature of the international exhibitions of 'manufacturing arts'. Many Western nations saw the advantages in displaying collections of foreign and ancient artifacts to stimulate designers and consumers alike. However, while earlier indigenous artifacts and new objects from international exhibitions were collected, recording and preserving contemporary or recent work were seldom major concerns. (Around the world these were instead held in royal and state repositories, as well as company archives, which in the closing decades of the 20th century became appreciated as 'neo-archaeological' in their comprehensive documentation of the relationships between place, time and technique.) For textiles – as for other media – this focused attention on non-Western and pre-industrial sources, to profound effect. Initially the influence was primarily stylistic, as the 1860s fascination with all things

198. Constructed in the early 1990s, the Gottlieb-Daimler Stadium in Stuttgart incorporates a Trevira membrane roof that covers 36,000 square metres (43,000 square yards). Trevira is a Germany-based specialist manufacturer of hi-tech polyester fibres and filaments.

199. The strikingly simple embroidery of Ann Macbeth (1875–1948) and others of the Glasgow School is represented by this detail of a 1908–10 silk-on-silk appliquéd curtain. While the motifs may be indebted to Japan, the effect also reflects nearer Eastern precedents such as the Ottoman-influenced Orthodox embroideries of the 16th century.

Japanese melded with the relatively recent taste for Ottoman patterns and the established use of Indian designs. Arts and Crafts textiles were heavily dependent upon these sources.

Meanwhile, museums had repositioned textiles as 'pictures' by presenting them as static, flat, non-textural objects, often framed. Embroiderers frequently subverted this concept to their own ends. By the 1890s flatness was a visual characteristic played with in broad swathes of colour, whether of smooth stitches or appliqué. An expanse of background cloth itself was once again allowed to 'speak' as part of the composition. Foremost among the early proponents of this approach were the women associated with the Glasgow School of Art, such as Jessie Newberry and Ann Macbeth. This group disseminated a distinct and widely influential Scottish Secessionist style, particularly through publications aimed at school teachers. The succeeding generation reacted to these composed, stained-glass-like panels with a freer exploration of stitch and appliqué, often exposing raw edges and emphasizing the collage process by using layered backing fabrics, the upper one transparent. Rebecca Crompton, particularly in her 1936 publication, *Modern Design in Embroidery*, promoted both this approach and the evolution of design as the work progressed, using stitch rather than pencil on paper (thus paralleling the notion of graver-as-pen). She also exploited the understanding that frames denoted 'importance', by customizing them.

One of a number of English women associated in the 1910s and 1920s with Derby College of Art (where Macbeth occasionally taught), Crompton's widely distributed 1933 booklet for

Dryad, *Plea for Freedom*, had lasting effects. So too did her work as the first advisor – from 1934 to 1940 and then from 1945 until her early death in 1947 – to the thread manufacturer J. P. Coat's influential Needlework Development Scheme (which was initiated in Scotland and ran until 1961) and her simultaneous collaboration with Singer to develop ideas for machine embroidery. Exhibitions including work by Derby embroiderers – which in the 1940s and 1950s toured widely in the United States, Canada, Italy, Africa, Australia, New Zealand and Hong Kong – were seminal in the worldwide postwar reassessment of stitch as an expressive medium. Crompton's provision of educational materials and short courses for teachers continued to have an impact through instructors such as Constance Howard, whose postwar contribution to this field lives on in the research centre carrying her name at Goldsmiths College, London. The very success of collaborations such as Crompton's presented challenges in the 1960s and 1970s, when thread and yarn manufacturers' kits burdened embroidery with a formulaic taint. Creative thinkers stepped around this by again reconsidering materials and methods; the placing of embroidery with 'pictures' was confronted and its separation from other fibre arts challenged.

Collecting by private individuals and museums had by the 1920s substantially altered attitudes towards textiles in both academic and practical terms, by exposing the West to other cultures, past and present, native and foreign. Archaeological digs, ethnographic expeditions, fact-finding missions and personal

200. Rebecca Crompton (1898–1947) made a substantial contribution to the worldwide development of 'free style' embroidery, with pieces such as this, made in England in about 1936. Entitled *Le printemps*, this detail of a large panel (120 x 183 centimetres, 4 x 6 feet) illustrates her double-layer technique, in which appliqué is overlaid with stitched net.

interests were equally influential. There emerged a growing recognition of what were then called the 'primitive' and 'peasant' arts, appreciated in part for their vocabulary of abstract symbols. Such collections inspired the 'naive' approach of Werkstätte and early Bauhaus designs – and the related 'art munichois', centred around Munich and its Bavarian past – while textiles of the Ainu, Maya and others were the lynch-pins by which several New York museums supported the development of a non-European American aesthetic from 1916 to 1922. Some ancient finds even created a stylistic vogue (as happened with the opening of Tutankhamon's tomb in 1922). Increasingly, however, makers with direct conduits to local minority or external cultures expressed a profound respect for the techniques themselves. These influences followed pre-existing strengths and spheres of interest. For example, the Dutch-sponsored demonstrations by Javanese batik specialists at the 1900 Paris international exhibition prompted its reassessment and dissemination. By the time of the 1925 'Art Deco' international exhibition (also in Paris), batik dominated the innovative displays of most exhibiting countries and was an important expressive vehicle in the United States as well. (Its use thereafter ebbed and flowed until the 1970s, when Japanese *rōzome* gained a substantial following in North America.) Simultaneously, French weavers had responded to a wide range of embroidered, woven and ikat-dyed cloths

20

202. After the First World War, Paul Rodier employed thousands of home-based weavers, spinners and embroiderers in northern France, producing cloths such as these, the largest having a linen ground tambour-worked in wool.

from their Pacific and African colonies, an *hommage* evident in the work of Rodier and Hélène Henry. To the north, Scandinavian and other traditional methods of rug weaving were revisited, a trend that would have worldwide repercussions as part of the postwar Scandinavian Modern style.

More pervasive was the impact of German excavations of Peruvian textiles, begun in the 1880s. These, along with Mesoamerican and especially Mexican examples, received sustained study in the interwar period from the likes of M. D. C. Crawford, from the New York museum-to-design campaign, and the French scholar Raoul d'Harcourt, who published groundbreaking weave analyses. Designers such as Ruth Reeves and, later, Anni Albers drew on first-hand knowledge of such textiles. Albers, today the best known Bauhaus weaver, directed attention to the sophistication of prehistoric Latin American weavers in her influential American publications of 1959 and 1965. She also amassed a sizeable number of pieces, now in public collections. In the process, such work showed that the upright tapestry loom of the Egyptians and Peruvians was similar to the tapestry and rug looms still used in Africa, Greece, the Middle East and among the Navajo. This is one example of the way collecting, scholarship and intuitive responses confronted the notion of the 'primitive' and instead celebrated other skills and cultures.

An earlier example of this respect can be found in the work of Ethel Mairet. While married to Ananda Coomaraswamy, and living in Sri Lanka, she collected textiles and absorbed aspects of that culture's ideology, which she combined with Arts & Crafts influences to define her subsequent commitment to 'noble simplicity' (and the 'three crafts') as aspects of a good life, as well as good work. Mairet's approach – admired by the potters Bernard

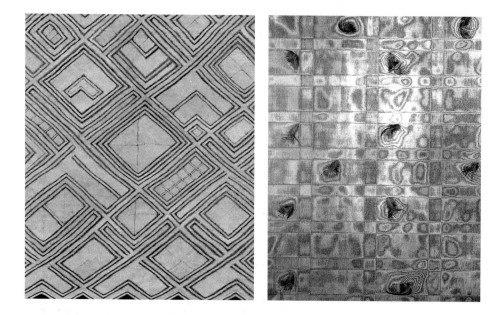

203. African arts had a profound influence on those of the West in the 20th century. Among the textiles, those particularly admired for their non-repeating patterns are the post-1860 raffia cut-pile embroidered cloths of the Tshokwe, from the Kasai region of the Congo.

204. Japan's Nuno Corporation is renowned for its innovative cloths. *Feather Flurries* has feathers trapped within a calendared silk 'pocket cloth' or double weave. It was designed in 1995 by Reiko Sudo, who co-founded the firm in 1984.

Leech and Hamada Shoji – influenced the Japanese Kokten Korgei, a coalition formed in 1927 to restore recognition of the rich tradition of indigenous craftsmanship, in opposition to the official policy of Westernization established in 1861 and the prevailing view that the crafts were inferior to painting and sculpture. By the 1960s Japanese cloth-designers had achieved worldwide acclaim, largely through the work of Junichi Arai and next-generation designers such as Reiko Sudo, who nurtured a variant of 'noble simplicity'. Yet Japanese architects and art museums still eschewed textiles until 1989, when Tokyo's National Museum of Art purchased its first example, Shigio Kubota's *The Wave Space II*. Only after this did Japanese corporate and public buildings begin to incorporate fibre arts.

In keeping with the contradictions sustained by textiles, recent institutionalized mechanisms dedicated to preserving skills and livelihoods – such as NGOs (non-governmental organizations), fair-trade organizations and indigenous state-supported cooperatives – have sometimes presented non-Western and tribal products as 'good works' while at the same time ensuring that they are exposed to the public as art. Such initiatives have their origins in the mid-19th century. This social history of textiles takes two forms, the first of which is self-initiated. It can be seen in the cloths of, for example, India and Latin America, which countered machine-made fabrics by handweaving machine-spun yarns or diversifying into more elaborate cloths, or in cultures such as those of western Africa and the Far East, where the narrow cloth width was imbedded in culturally significant clothing. The scarcity of earlier textiles leaves this transition open to analysis, but it appears that textiles became more elaborate under these circumstances. Certainly later in the West, the proliferation of upmarket, limited-run, single-commission, community-based and 'salvage' textiles coincided precisely with the loss of industrial dominance and subsequent incursion of imported textiles first in Britain from about 1890 (increasing markedly after the First World War) and then in the US from about 1970. (Today's industrial 'rising star' is China, with the world's greatest spinning capacity.)

In addition, the 20th-century narratives of non-Western textiles are in many cases (as in Africa and Latin America), confrontational to European legacies, subverting capitalist and even older tribute systems to sustain good lives by reasserting the relevance of textiles as a medium of employment, identity and parody. The most dramatic and effective use of this strategy was Mahatma Gandhi's mid-century proclamation urging Indians to return to their indigenous cloths and clothes to break the thrall of dependency on, and outward flow of cash to, European manufacturers. In so doing, he achieved exactly what European states had themselves done some two or three centuries before. Within Western societies a quieter anti-establishment movement emerged, counteracting the homogeneity of globalization with spirited pursuit of regional strengths, whether in Pacific rim arts (for example, in Australia and New Zealand), Iberian traditions (Spain), multilingual cultures (eastern Canada), or Baltic self-reliance (northeastern Europe).

The second form of 'good work' is externally initiated, and is today underwritten by organizations as diverse as the World Bank and Oxfam. Historically, this role was played by missionary and convent schools. The work of such institutions is not yet fully understood, and while they are frequently praised as enablers, they are also accused of being forces for colonialism. This sums up the underlying contradiction inherent in many cultural exchanges centred on textiles. Less still is known about the reverse influences, even as late as the 1960s and 1970s when it is thought that returning members of the Peace Corps contributed substantially to the 'discovery' of several shibori techniques in the United States (especially tie-and-dye). During the same decades basket-making and related off-loom tech-

205. A young Ghanaian woman outside church in Kumasi on Sunday morning wears 'Dutch wax' (resin resist) cloth that incorporates images of sewing machines into its pattern. The trade in such machine-batik printed fabrics (long imported from England and Holland, but now increasingly produced in Africa) is largely controlled by West African women, the most successful of whom are call 'Mama Benzis' after Mercedes-Benz cars and other symbols of wealth.

206. The Victorian Tapestry Workshop was founded by that Australian state's government in 1976 and has since contributed not only to the revival of tapestry but to the wider exposure of Aboriginal arts, as in *Awelye II* (1994–5) by Gloria Petyarre.

niques entered a sustained period of innovation, providing telling insights into the ongoing dialogue between diverse cultures, philanthropic intervention, 'outsider' reassessment of established textile techniques, and self-initiated renewal.

Less contentious are the philanthropic agencies or individuals that aimed at alleviating the iniquities within social boundaries rather than across them. The work of Candice Wheeler through Associated Artists (New York, 1883–1907) is one example, as are the many projects induced by the Depression, including those administered by the Works Progress Administration (1935–42) throughout the United States and initiated by smaller organizations both there and elsewhere. Out of the latter period came a lasting recognition of quilt-making as a significant expression of communal ideologies, whether based on region, ethnic background or gender. For women in the period after the Second World War, stitch and appliqué became potent politicizing tools, whether the result was displayed or worn. This use goes back to the banners, rosettes and sashes of early 20th-century Suffragettes, behind which lay the Art Needlework movement that emerged in Britain during the 1870s. Epitomized by the Royal School of Needlework (founded in London in 1872 as the School of Art Needlework), the Art Needlework movement's distinct approach was based on freely chosen shading and the extensive use of appliqué, as well as a desire to train 'gentlewomen in reduced circumstances'. Such training and philosophy were inspired by the principles of self-help and the embroidery techniques of sisterhoods who through convent workrooms several decades before had begun

207. *Losing our memory* (1999) by Dutch textile artist Tilleke Schwarz (b. 1946) calls forth the universal role of textiles as carriers of messages. The stitched imagery and texts highlight the danger posed by erased, outdated or corrupted digital information to the human need to communicate and create histories.

208. This altar frontal, designed by the English architect J. D. Sedding, was embroidered in 1869 by the Society of St Margaret, East Grinstead, under the supervision of the designer's sister, herself a member of this Anglo-Catholic order. Their embroidery schools, including one in London (1870–1902, then run independently) and a daughter house in Boston, Massachusetts, helped to disseminate the free-interpretation approach seen in this detail.

to influence Anglican liturgical practices and instituted local social and educational reforms (ultimately applied throughout the British Empire and elsewhere). All of these were essentially domestic enterprises. The principle they held in common was 'for women, by women' and they capitalized on readily accessible spaces – home, church, the streets – long before galleries and museums opened their doors to such socio-political art.

Typically, in their exploratory stages, new techniques were and are most often disseminated by women, who around the world play a dominant role in textile education and guilds, societies and formally constituted networks. Such risk-taking in the margins sometimes compounded rather than reduced influence. Screen-printing, for example, was not recognized as an art form on paper until the late 1930s, a decade or so after many trained in graphic and fine arts – again mainly women – had applied it to textiles. In the last quarter of the 20th century the implementation of computer-aided design systems was similarly led by innovators on the fringes of the industry. For this reason, most influential makers and designers remain anonymous in the global sense, even if individuals become acknowledged within their own sphere. Standing in opposition to the consumers who since the 1950s had come to rely increasingly on institutional approval (ranging from juried exhibitions to 'branding' by association with influential schools, publications or even firms), being unseen has been relished by those who manoeuvred through the maze of art/craft/industry to reach their own goals. Such satisfaction goes straight to the heart of textiles as an

intimate expression. In global terms it is represented by the Jack Lenor Larson company's reputation for innovation and creative support of indigenous skills, behind which lay the unpublicized but significant contribution made by Win Anderson between 1961 and 1976: in a happy collaboration, he facilitated and she wove the prototypes for production around the world.

At times lip-service has been paid to many makers by calling them artists (a peculiarly Western concept especially prevalent in North America) and the uneasy relationship between fine and applied arts evident in 1850 has not yet been resolved, nor should it be. Of all media, textiles have thrived most on the freedom found in the spaces between the established and experimental, the public and private, tradition and innovation, and beauty and utility. These dualities have been a great stimulus around the world, and especially appropriate to women every-

209. Judit Kárpáti-Rácz (b. 1973) is the only person worldwide to use the traditional Hungarian hair-knotting technique *lószörfonás* at much greater scale and with materials such as metal wire, plastic cord or nylon monofilament. Since perfecting the approach in 1996, she has used it to create objects ranging from bowls to 'backbags'.

210. By the early 21st century, the most powerful textiles were referenced from textiles rather than other arts. Michael Brennand-Wood (b. 1952) has been highly infuential in this respect, through both short courses from Britain to Japan and works such as *Around and Around* (1997). In this case he draws inspiration from *reticella* laces and a 'rediscovery' of print-block making techniques.

where, whose social roles most frequently demand negotiation between these and other opposing forces. This facility has also allowed 'outsider' textiles of the sorts outlined above – made by both men and women – to defy conventions and take risks with new or revisited hand-production techniques. Textiles have at times contributed directly to philosophies of art (such as those formulated in the later 19th century by Alois Riegl) and art movements such as Neo-Expressionism (a term first applied to German art during the 1980s). This rejected minimalism and instead celebrated texture, emotion, sexuality and narrative – the very themes that propelled central and eastern European fibre arts with such impact into the textile world during the 1960s and 1970s and that have defined many textile approaches since. By the 1990s, many of the arts dealing with autobiography and memory drew on textiles or their techniques, since these, with a history far longer and more inclusive than any other artifact, provide universal and ancient metaphors for life and human origins. Computer-crunched fractal analysis today confirms what textile mythologies have always maintained: that life is based on patterns, spun out in potentially never-ending repetitions until the structure is in accord with its destiny.

Glossary

acetate See CELLULOSE

acids Chemical compounds containing hydrogen that can be replaced by a metal atom to produce a SALT; they turn litmus red. Weak acids occur naturally in vinegar, citrus fruit, milk and insect-reds such as kermes and cochineal. Their pH is low.

acrylic See SYNTHETIC FIBRES

alizarin ($C14 H6 O2(OH)2$) A widely occurring orange-red crystalline solid extracted from many dye roots including madder and other species of *Rubia*, Indian chay, Asian morinda and Latin American *Relbunium*; now made from the coal-tar derivative anthracine and yielding a wide variety of dyes.

alkalis Compounds (bases) that react with ACIDS to form SALTS and water and, specifically, dissolve in water; they turn litmus blue. Alkalis are important in reducing insoluble dyestuffs into solution, both in immersion and DRY/COLD DYEING. Alkali metals include sodium and potassium; alkaline earth metals include calcium and magnesium. Their pH is high.

alum See SALTS

appliqué The stitching of a piece of cloth onto a ground fabric; reverse appliqué employs two layers of cloth with the top one cut into to reveal the one below; *molas* are made with three or more layers; in *intarsia* two layers are cut simultaneously, one for the ground and the other for the pattern.

arras See TAPESTRY

bahda See RESISTS

bast Formerly denoting the inner bark of the linden (lime) tree, bast now refers to any flexible fibrous bark and, with their similar cellular structures, to all woody PLANT FIBRES.

batik See RESISTS

bowing See CARDING

brocading See WEFT

buratto Pattern-darned knotted netting, also called lacis; similar to filet, which is darning on twined net.

camelid Fibres from the *Camelidae* family, which includes camels, alpaca and llama; these are PROTEIN FIBRES.

carpets See COMPOUND CLOTH, WARP

cartoon See TAPESTRY

carding Cross-combing of fibres to remove debris, to fluff and to prepare into slivers (bundles of fibres) for spinning; also achieved by 'bowing' with, as the term implies, a hunting-type bow rotated end-on amid the fibres.

cashmere A PROTEIN FIBRE from the underbelly of the Kashmir goat, now produced mainly in China, Mongolia and Iran.

cellulose ($C6 H10 O5$) A carbohydrate that is an important constituent of the cell walls of plants; for acetates, viscose and related regenerated fibres it is obtained from wood pulp. It is destroyed by strong ACIDS.

chay See ALIZARIN

chintz A multifaceted term attributed to corruptions from various Indian words, mainly *chitta*, meaning spotted or coloured; by the 18th century meaning a full-colour smooth printed cotton (limited palettes were called 'demi-chintzes'). Also denoting a high-gloss finish and, among some weavers, use of supplementary colouring WEFTS.

cochineal See ACIDS, MORDANT

colourant A semi-permanent or permanent staining substance, binding physically or chemically with the cloth.

combing Preparing fibres by aligning them rather than cross-combing; the resulting rovings (bundles of fibres) produce a smoother yarn.

compound cloth Used here to indicate the wide range of cloths made by incorporating WARPS and/or WEFTS beyond those needed for a structurally sound fabric, generally to introduce more elaborate patterns (and therefore 'figured') or make thicker cloths/carpets such as doublecloth and triplecloth.

cotton See PLANT FIBRES

couching Securing threads or other decorative elements with another thread.

damask Any fabric figured solely through the juxtaposition of two weave structures, typically SATIN and TWILL.

denim See TWILL

discharge The method of creating a pattern by bleaching selected areas – technically, a DRY/COLD DYEING process.

distaff See DRAFT SPINNING

draft spinning Combining fibres by simultaneously drawing out a bundle to produce a continuous strand and twisting the strand to secure the fibres together. The basic tools are something to hold the bundle of fibres (a distaff) and something to maintain the spin and hold the spun yarns (a spindle, often dropped and weighted like a top with a whorl or, later, propelled by a wheel). See ill. 41.

drawloom See TRUE LOOM

dry/cold dyeing Any aspect of pattern-dyeing that does not involve immersion or steaming, even though immersion may precede or follow the procedure.

esparto See PLANT FIBRES

faced weaves See PLAIN WEAVE, SATIN, TAPESTRY, TWILL, WARP

figured See COMPOUND CLOTH

filet See BURATTO

fly-shuttle A hand operated sling-like device to propel the shuttle in one stroke from selvedge to selvedge.

gauze A loom-made openwork cloth based on twisted adjacent WARPS held in place by the WEFT before twisting back to rest; related to sprang (which has no binding wefts) and warp-twining (which does not twist back).

heddle The component of a TRUE LOOM through which WARPS pass so that they can be lifted, whether individually (as in TAPESTRY and related handweaving techniques) or in predetermined groups. Initially composed of string looped around a rod, it evolved into eyed strings between two bars and later was made of metal, when the ensemble became known as a 'shaft' or 'harness'.

herringbone See TWILL

ikat See RESISTS

indican The principal dye compound found in the leaves of tropical indigo plants, nearly identical to that in the leaves of woad and a constituent of the shellfish dye, murex. Fermentation of indican produces indoxyl, which bonds around fibres to create the most permanent of dyes.

indigo See INDICAN

Jacquard See TRUE LOOM

jean See TWILL

kelim See TAPESTRY

kermes See ACID, MORDANT

kesi See TAPESTRY

kosode Long Japanese garment with small wrist opening worn up to the late 19th century.

lac See MORDANT

lacis See BURATTO

linen Both the yarn and the cloth made from the PLANT FIBRES flax and hemp.

madder See ALIZARIN, MORDANT

metal threads These include flat gilt membrane, gilt wire, or paper wrapped around a fibre core; often brittle and unable to withstand tension, they are used in weaving solely as WEFT threads and secured in embroidery by COUCHING.

mohair A PROTEIN FIBRE of relatively long, white lustrous hair with no felting properties, from the angora goat native to Asia Minor.

mola See APPLIQUÉ

moquette See WARP

mordant A chemical agent (often a metallic SALT) that forms an insoluble bond between fibres and dyes. Different mordants produce different colours with the same dye, a method so effective with red dyes that it was once called the 'madder style'. ALIZARIN, cochineal, kermes and lac are all mordant dyes.

morinda See ALIZARIN

murex See INDICAN

ochres Natural COLOURANTS of hydrated ferric oxide with impurities, a type of limonite deposit derived from weathering of minerals containing iron. Limonites range in colour from yellow to red, brown and black and occur in bog iron ore, gossan and tropical and sub-tropical laterites.

pH A number from 1 to 14 representing a logarithmic scale with pH 7 being neutral; below that the substance contains increasing amounts of ACID and above, ALKALIS.

paillettes Small shiny objects of, or with the appearance of, gilt, silvered or coloured metal, also called spangles and sequins.

plain weave Also called 'tabby'; the simplest weave construction, consisting of alternating over–under passes of a WEFT. In balanced plain weaves the weft and WARP diameters are identical or similar; in faced weaves the 'face' yarn is finer than the buried one.

plangi See RESISTS

plant fibres The largest group of natural fibres, composed largely of CELLULOSE and including: cotton; BASTS such as flax, hemp and nettles including ramie; grasses, palm vines and leaves; rushes and reeds such as esparto and papyrus; and pulped leaves such as yucca and sisal.

plying See SPINDLE WHEEL

Prehistoric Southwest A large area in the United States with close connections to cultures across the present-day boundary with Mexico.

polyester See SYNTHETIC FIBRES

protein fibres Complex organic compounds consisting of one or more chains of amino acids linked by peptide bonds (-NH-CO-) and manufactured by cells. One, keratin, is an insoluble fibrous protein and is the major constituent of silk and all mammalian coats, whether called hair, wool or fur. They are destroyed by ALKALIS.

radiocarbon dating Measures the constant and steady decay of radioactive Carbon 14 and is used for dating organic matter less than 40,000 years old.

ramie See PLANT FIBRES

regenerated fibres See CELLULOSE

Relbunium See ALIZARIN

resists Physical resists (shibori) use thread bindings (*bahda, plangi*, tie-and-dye, or tie-dyeing), clamps or any other device to apply pressure to certain areas of cloth (or yarn, in ikat) so that dyestuffs cannot penetrate; they are designed for immersion dyeing.

Additive resists have paste, mud or wax added to the surface of the cloth and are used for immersion (batik, *rōzome*) and for DRY/COLD DYEING (*rōzuri*).

roving See COMBING

rōzome/rōzuri See RESISTS

salts Sodium chloride (NaCl) and any similar compound such as alum, formed, together with water, when an ACID reacts with a base; important in MORDANTS and in making many things including soap, fertilizer and ceramics.

samitum See TWILL

satin A weave construction with long floats giving a glossy surface, typically WARP-faced.

serge See TWILL

shabrak An ornamental horsecloth.

shibori See RESISTS

silk See PROTEIN FIBRES, SPINDLE WHEEL

sliver See CARDING

spindle wheel This drives a spindle by hand or treadle to combine threads together ('throwing' in silks, 'plying' when combining two or more ready-prepared yarns); bobbins are also wound on a similar wheel.

spinning wheel This has various forms all designed for DRAFT SPINNING.

splicing To unite by lapping ends and twisting.

sprang See GAUZE

synthetic fibres Generally, fibres such as polyester and acrylic that are made by obtaining or creating polymers, which are modified for use as fibres, thermoplastics and paints.

tambour work Chain stitch worked with crook-end needle or tambour hook.

tapestry Generally, when handwoven, a WEFT-faced construction in which the WARP is entirely covered by threads worked back and forth only in the area where they are needed; terms used to describe this technique include *kesi* (in silk, also called *k'o-ssu*) *kemao* (in wool), *tsuzure-ori* (Japanese for 'fingernail weave'), arras (after Arras and giving the Italian *arazzi*) and kelim (although the latter in Turkish and Polish means both flat-woven and knotted carpets). TWILL-tapestry is so named to identify the weave structure, which is otherwise plain. The drawings for tapestries are called 'cartoons'. The term tapestry is also used among power-weavers to denote weft-intensive cloths or anything that resembles tapestry in the complexity of its pattern, as in carpets made with printed WARPS.

tartan See TWILL

throwing See SPINDLE WHEEL

tie-and-dye See RESISTS

tiputas Poncho-like garments made of paper-thin layers of tapa (bark cloth).

tissue See WEFT

Transylvanian A style of carpet associated with Transylvania, a self-governing Romanian princedom within the Ottoman empire until 1687 when it became part of the Holy Roman Empire.

trapunto Localized padding inserted in slits in the back of quilted fabrics.

true loom Any weaving machine with a systematic means of creating an opening (shed) for the WEFT, called an automatic shedding device; this includes the shed rod, HEDDLE rods, and complex technologies such as the drawloom and the Jacquard. See ills 23, 36, 38, 60, 77, 182.

turnsole An annual euphorbiaceous plant giving a MORDANT dye; also well known among illuminators and later widely used as a food colour.

twill A range of weave constructions producing a diagonal line and described according to the number of WARP and WEFT threads involved; they include serge (*sergé* is the French for twill), true tartan, denim, jean and *samitum* (or samite, 1:2 weft-faced twill). Herringbone is a twill reversed at regular points to form a chevron.

velvet/velveteen See WARP, WEFT

viscose See CELLULOSE

warp The tensioned threads in loom weaving, also called 'end'. Weaves showing more warp than WEFT are called 'warp-faced'. The pile in velvet, moquette, Wilton (cut moquette), Brussels (uncut moquette) and Tapestry Brussels (printed warp) is formed by a supplementary warp that is looped temporarily over a weft-ways rod and secured by several ground wefts; the loops are cut open or left looped and the rod is removed. See ills 182, 183.

warp-twining See GAUZE

weft The non-tensioned threads in loom weaving, also called 'pick'. Wefts running from selvedge to selvedge that are additional to those required for the cloth's structure and predominantly on the cloth face are called 'supplementary wefts' or, if less apparent, 'tissuing wefts' (hence the cloth term, 'tissue'). The hand insertion of localized wefts is brocading. Weaves with all or much of the warp covered are called 'weft-faced'. The pile in velveteen is formed by looped and cut supplementary wefts.

whorl See DRAFT SPINNING

woad See INDICAN

wool, woollen, worsted These denote differences in spinning. Early hard-twisted hand-spun fibres are wool, itself a PROTEIN FIBRE; wool and all other soft-CARDED, wheel-spun fibres are described as woollen-spun; COMBED fibres are worsted-spun.

Select Bibliography

Chapter 1

Beyond Tradition: Lao Textiles Revisited (The Handwoven Textiles of Carol Cassidy), New York, 1995

Barber, E., Women's Work: The First 20,000 Years, New York, 1994

Bobart, H. H., Basketwork through the Ages, [1st ed. 1936] London, 1997

Braun, B. (ed.), Arts of the Amazon, New York and London, 1995

Collingwood, P., The Techniques of Rug Weaving, [1973] New York and London, 1999

——, The Techniques of Sprang, New York and London, 1974

Conway, S., Thai Textiles, London, 1992

Emery, I., The Primary Structure of Fabrics: An Illustrated Classification, [1966] London and New York, 1995

Fisch, A. M., Textile Techniques in Metal, North Carolina, 1996

Gillow, J., and B. Sentance, World Textiles: A Visual Guide to Traditional Techniques, London, 1999

MacKenzie, M. A., Androgynous Objects: String Bags and Gender in Central New Guinea: Studies in Anthropology and History, vol. 2, [1991] Melbourne, 1998

Rossbach, E., Baskets as Textile Art, London, 1974

Seiler-Baldinger, A., Textiles: Classification of Techniques, Bathurst, Australia, 1994

Sentance, B., Basketry: A World Guide to Traditional Techniques, London, 2001

Wild, J. P., Textiles in Archaeology, Shire Archaeology 56, Aylesbury, 1988

Chapter 2

Balfour-Paul, J., Indigo, London, 1998

Barber, E., Prehistoric Textiles, Princeton, 1991

Chenciner, R., Madder Red: A History of Luxury and Trade, Richmond, 2000

Forbes, R. J., Studies in Ancient Technology. vol. 3: Paints and Pigments, [1964] Leiden, 1993; vol. 4: Fibres and Fabrics, [1964] Leiden, 1987

Geijer, A., A History of Textile Art, London, 1979

Gillow, J., Printed and Dyed Textiles from Africa, London, 2001

Hald, M., Ancient Danish Textiles from Bogs and Burials, Archaeological-Historical Series, vol. 21, Copenhagen, 1980

Hoffmann, M., The Warp-weighted Loom, [1974] McMinnille, Oregon, 1997

Kasselman, K. D., Natural Dyes of the Asia Pacific Region, Studio Vista Monograph Series, vol. 2, London, 1997

Konieczny, M. G., Textiles of Baluchistan, London, 1979

Lamb, V. and L., Sierra Leone Weaving, Hertingford, Herts., 1984

Pancake, C. M., and S. Baizerman, 'Guatemalan Gauze Weaves: A Description and Key to Identification', Textile Museum Journal 19–20, Washington, D.C., 1980–81

Rogers, P. W., and J. Kirby (eds) Dyes in History and Archaeology, London, 1982

Rowe, A. P., Costumes and Featherwork of the Lords of Chimor: Textiles from Peru's North Coast, Washington, D.C., 1984

Sandberg, G., The Red Dyes: Cochineal, Madder, and Murex Purple, [1994] North Carolina, 1997

Vavalle, J. A. de, and J. A. G. Garcia, The Textile Arts of Peru, [1989] Lima, 1993

Chapter 3

Becker, J., Pattern and Loom: A Practical Study of the Development of Weaving Techniques in China, Western Asia and Europe, Copenhagen, 1987

Debaine-Francfort, C., and A. Idriss, Keriya mémoires d'un fleuve: Archéologie et des oasis du Talkamakan, Suilly-la-Tour, 2000

Edmunds, J., Tyrian or Imperial Purple Dye, Little Chalfont, Bucks., England, 2000

Jenkins, D. (ed.), The Cambridge History of Western Textiles, Cambridge, 2003

Koslin, D., 'Between the Empirical and the Rational: Looms through Time and Space' in M. Schoeser, C. Boydell (eds) Disentangling Textiles, London, 2003

Rivers, V. Z., The Shining Cloth: Dress and Adornment that Glitters, London, 1999

Sawyers, A. R., Early Nasca Needlework, London, 1997

Sheng, A., 'The Origin of Chinese Tapestry Weave: a New Hypothesis', Textile History 26:1, Leeds, spring 1995

Stauffer, A., Textiles of Late Antiquity, New York, 1995

Trilling, J., Roman Heritage: Textiles from Egypt and Eastern Mediterranean 300–600 AD, Washington, D.C., 1982

Zhao, F., Treasures in Silk: An Illustrated History of Chinese Textiles, 1999

Chapter 4

Ancient and Medieval Textiles: Studies in Honour of Donald King, Textile History 20:2, Leeds, Autumn 1989

Special Issue on Medieval Textiles, Textile History 32:1, Leeds, May 2001

Allsen, T. T., Commodity and Exchange in the Mongol Empire: A Cultural History of Islamic Textiles, Cambridge, 2001

Bonar, E. H. (ed.), Woven by the Grandmothers: Nineteenth Century Navajo Textiles from the National Museum of the American Indian, Washington, D.C., 1996

Brown, C., et al., Weaving China's Past: The Amy S Clague Collection of Chinese Textiles, Phoenix, Ariz., 2000

Drooker, P. B., and L. D. Webster (eds), Beyond Cloth and Cordage: Archaeological Textile Research in the Americas, Salt Lake City, 2000

Erikson, M., Textiles in Egypt 200–1500 AD in Swedish Museums, Göteborg, 1997

Gittinger, M., Splendid Symbols: Textiles and Tradition in Indonesia, [1979] Singapore and New York, 1990

Jackson, B., and D. Hugus, Ladder to the Clouds: Intrigue and Tradition in Chinese Rank, Berkeley, 1999

Kent, K. P., Prehistoric Textiles of the Southwest, Albuquerque, N. M., 1983

Liu, X., Silk and Religion: An Exploration of Material Life and the Thought of People, AD 600–1200, Delhi, 1998

Munro, J. H., Textiles, Towns and Trade, Aldershot, Hants, 1994

Rowe, A. P. (ed.), Costume and Identity in Highland Ecuador, Washington, D.C. and Seattle, Wash., 1998

Scott, P., The Book of Silk, [1993] London, 2001

Teague, L. S., Textiles in Southwestern Prehistory, Alburquerque, N. M., 1998

Thomas, T. K., and D. G. Harding, Textiles from Medieval Egypt, AD 300–1300, Pittsburgh, 1990

Tozer, A., Threads of Imagination: Central Asian and Chinese Silks from the 12th to the 19th Century, London, 1999

Weiner A. B., and J. Schneider (eds), Cloth and Human Experience, [1989] Washington, D.C. and London, 1991

Chapter 5

German Renaissance Patterns for Embroidery: A Facsimile Copy of Nicolas Bassee's New Modelbuch of 1568, Austin, 1994

Bridgeman, H., and E. Drury (eds), Needlework: An Illustrated History, London and New York, 1978

Carlano, M., and L. Salmon (eds), French Textiles, Hartford, Conn., 1985

Cavallo, A., Medieval Tapestries in the Metropolitan Museum of Art, New York, 1993

Crowfoot, E., F. Pritchard and K. Staniland, Textiles and Clothing: 1150–1450, Woodbridge, Suff., 2001

Delmarcel, G., Flemish Tapestries from the 15th to the 18th Century, Tielt, 1999

Fanelli, R. Bonito, Five Centuries of Italian Textiles, 1300–1800: A Selection from the Museo Tessuto Prato, Prato, 1981

Marinis, F. de', Velvet: History, Techniques, Fashion, Milan, 1994

May, F. L., Silk Textiles of Spain: Eighth to Fifteenth Century, New York, 1957

Miller, L., 'Paris-Lyon-Paris' in R. Fox, A. Turner, Luxury Trades and Consumerism in Ancien Régime Paris, Aldershot, 1998

Phillips, B., Tapestry, London, 1994

Schoeser, M., French Textiles 1760 to the Present Day, London and Paris, 1991

Staniland, K., Medieval Craftsmen: Embroiderers, London, 1991

Vega, P. Junquera de and C. H. Carretero, Catálogo de Tapices, Madrid, 1986

Chapter 6

The Fabric of Their Lives: Hooked and Poked Mats of Newfoundland and Labrador, St John's, Newf., 1980

Bier, C., Persian Velvets at Rosenborg, Copenhagen, 1995

Ellis, M., Embroideries and Samplers from Islamic Egypt, Oxford, 2001

Fisher, N. (ed.), Rio Grande Textiles, [1979] Santa Fe, N. M., 1994

Frances, M., Great Embroideries of Bukhara, London, 2000

Gervers, V., The Influence of Ottoman Turkish Textiles and Costume in Eastern Europe, Ontario, 1979

Hubel, R. G., Book of Carpets, New York, 1971

Huli, A., and J. Luczyc-Wyhowska, Kilim: The Complete Guide, London, 1993

Jackson, R. D., Imperial Silks: Ch'ing Dynasty Textiles in the Minneapolis Museum of Art, Minneapolis, 2000

MacAulay, S. P., *Stitching Rites: Colcha Embroidery among the Northern Rio Grande*, Tucson, 2000
Mayén, G., L. Asturias de Barrios and R. Miralbes de Polanco, *Corfadia: Mayan Ceremonial Clothing from Guatemala*, Museo Ixchel, Guatemala, 1993
Milanesi, E., *Carpet: Origins, Art and History*, Milan, 1999
Paine, S., *Embroidered Textiles: Traditional Patterns from Five Continents*, London, 1995
Raby, J., and A. Effeny (eds), *IPEK. The Crescent and the Rose: Imperial Ottoman Silks and Velvets*, London, 2001
Sherrill, S. B., *Carpets and Rugs of Europe and America*, New York, London, Paris, 1996
Spring, C., and J. Hudson, *North African Textiles*, Washington, D.C., 1995
Taylor, R., *Ottoman Embroidery*, New York, 1993
Wertime, J. T., *Sumak Bags of Northwest Persia and Transcaucasia*, London, 1998

Chapter 7

Barnes, R. R., *Indian Block-Printed Textiles in Egypt: The Newberry Collection in the Ashmolean Museum*, Oxford, 1997
Corrigan, G., *Miao Textiles from China*, London, 2001
Crill, R., *Indian Ikat Textiles*, London, 1998
Dronsfield, A., and J. Edmunds, *The Transition from Natural to Synthetic Dyes*, Little Chalfont, Bucks., 2001
Fox, R., and A. Nieto-Galen (eds), *Natural Dyestuffs and Industrial Culture in Europe 1750–1880*, Canton, Mass., 1999
Garfield, S., *Mauve: How One Man Invented a Colour that Changed the World*, London, 2000
Gibbon, K. F., and A. Hale, *Ikat Silks of Central Asia: The Guido Goldman Collection*, London, 1997
Gittinger, M., *Master Dyers to the World: Technique and Trade in Early Indian Dyed Cotton Textiles*, [1982] Washington, D.C., 1997
——, *Textiles and the Tai Experience in Southeast Asia*, Washington, D.C., 1992
Gluckman, D. C., and S. S. Takeda, *When Art Became Fashion: Kosode in Edo-period Japan*, Los Angeles and New York, 1992
Gonick, G., *Splendor of the Dragon: Costume of the Ryukyu Kingdom*, Los Angeles, 1995
Guy, J., *Woven Cargoes: Indian Textiles in the East*, London, 1998
Hamilton, R. W., *From the Rainbow's Varied Hue: Textiles of the Southern Philippines*, Los Angeles, 1998
Harvey, J., *Traditional Textiles of Central Asia*, London, 1996
Iwamoto Wada, Y., M. Kellogg Rice and J. Barton, *Shibori: The Inventive Art of Japanese Shaped Resist Dyeing*, [1983] Tokyo, New York, London, 1999
Neich, R., and M. Pendergrast, *Traditional Tapa Textiles of the Pacific*, London, 1997
Yoshioka, S., et al. (eds) *Tsutsugaki Textiles of Japan: Traditional Freehand Paste Resist Indigo Dyeing Technique of Auspicious Motifs*, Kyoto, 1987

Chapter 8

Askar, N., and R. Crill, *Colours of the Indus: Costumes and Textiles of Pakistan*, London, 1997
Dillmont, T. de, *The Complete Encyclopedia of Needlework*, [1891] Philadelphia, 1978
Durrie, A. J., *The Scottish Linen Industry in the Eighteenth Century*, Edinburgh, 1979
Fox, R., and A. Nieto-Galen (eds), *Natural Dyestuffs and Industrial Culture in Europe, 1750–1880*, Canton, Mass., 1999
Kiracofe, R., and M. E. Johnson, *American Quilt: A History of Cloth and Comfort 1750–1950*, New York, 1993
Levey, S. M., *Lace: A History*, London, 1983
Paludan, C., and L. de Hemmer Engeberg, *98 Monsterboger til Broderi, Knipling og Strikning (98 Pattern Books for Embroidery, Lace and Knitting)*, Copenhagen, 1991
Perrin, M., *Magnificent Molas: The Art of the Kuna Indians*, London, 1999
Rose, M. (ed.), *The Lancashire Cotton Industry: A History since 1700*, Preston, 1996
Rutt, R., *A History of Hand Knitting*, London, 1987
Schoeser, M., and C. Rufey, *English and American Textiles: 1790 to the Present Day*, London and New York, 1989
Thomas, G. Z., *Richer Than Spices*, New York, 1965
Tirthanhai, R. (ed.), *Cloth and Commerce: Textiles in Colonial India*, New Delhi and London, 1996
Zaman, N., *The Art of Kantha Embroidery*, [1981] Dhaka, Bangladesh, 1993

Chapter 9

Black, S., *Knitwear in Fashion*, London, 2002
Brackman, B., *Patterns of Progress: Quilts in the Machine Age*, Seattle, 1998
Earnshaw, P., *Lace Machines and Machine Laces*, London, 1986
Endrei, W., *The First Hundred Years of European Textile Printing*, Budapest, 1998
Handley, S., *Nylon: The Story of a Fashion Revolution*, Baltimore, 1999
Henderson, W. O., *The Industrialization of Europe 1780–1914*, London, 1969
Levitt, S., *Victorians Unbuttoned: Registered Designs for Clothing, their Makers and Wearers, 1839–1900*, London, Boston, Sydney, 1986
McCarty, C., and M. McQuaid, *Structure and Surface: Contemporary Japanese textiles*, New York, 1998
Noteboom, E., 'Screen Printing: Where Did it All Begin?', *Screenprinting 82/10*, Sept. 1992
Schoeser, M., *Fabrics and Wallpapers*, London and New York, 1986
Stevens, R. A. T., *Technology as Catalyst: Textile Artists on the Cutting Edge*, Washington, D.C., 2002
Wee, H. van der, *The Rise and Decline of Urban Industries in Italy and the Low Countries*, Leuven, 1988
Wells, F. A., *The British Hosiery and Knitwear Industry: Its History and Organisation*, London, 1972

Chapter 10

Coatts, M., *A Weaver's Life: Ethel Mairet 1872–1952*, London, 1983
Freeman, R. L., *Communion of the Spirits: African–American Quilters, Preservers, and Their Stories*, Nashville, Tenn., 1996
Gillow, J. and C. Iley, *Arts and Crafts of India*, London, 1996
Hanson, V., *Swedish Textile Art*, London, 1996
Hedlund, A. L., *Reflections of the Weaver's World: The Gloria F Ross Collection of Contemporary Navajo Weaving*, Denver and Seattle, 1992
Parry, L., *Textiles of the Arts and Crafts Movement*, London, 1988
Picton, J. (ed.), *The Art of African Textiles: Technology, Tradition and Lurex*, London, 1995
—— and J. Mack, *African Textiles*, London, 1980
Riegl, A., *Problems of Style: Foundation for the History of Ornament*, Princeton, 1993
Ross, D. H., *Wrapped in Pride: Ghanaian, Kente and African American Identity*, Los Angeles, 1998
Rowe, A. P., and J. Cohen, *Hidden Threads of Peru: Q'ero textiles*, Washington, D.C., 2002
Schoeser, M., *Bold Impressions: Block Printing 1910–1950*, London, 1995
—— (ed.), *The Watts Book of Embroidery: English Church Embroidery 1833–1953*, London, 1998
Stevens, R., and Y. Wada, *The Kimono Inspiration: Art and art-to-wear in America*, Washington DC, 1996
Troy, V. G., *Anni Albers and Ancient American Textiles: From Bauhaus to Black Mountain*, Aldershot, Hants, and Burlington, Vt., 2002
Völker, A., *Textiles of the Wiener Werkstätte 1910–1932*, London, 1994
Yunoki, Prof., et al., *The Japanese Craft Tradition: Kokten Korgei*, Blackwell, 2001

Bibliographies and reference

Blakeley, B. B., 'Recent developments in Chu studies: A Bibliographic and Institutional Overview', *Early China*, 1985–7
Clugston, M. J., *The New Penguin Dictionary of Science*, Harmondsworth, 1998
Daintith, J., *Oxford Dictionary of Chemistry*, Oxford, 2000
Hayward, J., et al., *The Cassell Atlas of World History*, London, 1997
Johnson, D. C., *Agile Hands and Creative Minds: A Bibliography of Textile Traditions in Afghanistan, Bangladesh, Bhutan, India, Nepal, Pakistan and Sri Lanka*, Bangkok, 2000
Randall, J. L., and E. M. Shook, *Bibliography of Mayan Textiles*, Guatemala City, 1993
Siegelaub, S. (ed.), *Bibliographica Textilia Historiae*, Amsterdam and New York, 1997
Tortora, P., and R. Muhel, *Fairchild's Dictionary of Textiles*, 7th ed., New York, 1996
Trench, L. (ed.), *Materials and Techniques in the Decorative Arts: An illustrated dictionary*, London, 2000

Acknowledgments for Illustrations

CI: Christie's Images, London
DB: Collection David Bernstein, New York
MS: Collection Mary Schoeser (Photo George Shiffner)
PMA: Philadelphia Museum of Art

1 CI. 2 PMA. Purchased with the Joseph E. Temple Fund. 1906-151. 3 Collection Victoria Z. Rivers. Photo Barbara Robin Molloy. 4 CI. 5 Musée de l'Homme, Paris. 6 © Xavier Renauld/Fondation EDF. 7 MS. 8–10 CI. 11 Peabody Museum, Harvard University, Cambridge, Mass. 12 CI. 13 © Xavier Renauld/Fondation EDF. 14 Photo IPAX. 15 © Museum der Kulturen, Basel. 16 University Museum, Philadelphia. 17 CI. 18 CI. 19 Abbot Hall Art Gallery, Kendal. 20 Photo courtesy of J. Mellaart. 21 MS. 22 Museo del Oro, Bogotá. 23 Metropolitan Museum of Art, New York. 24 CI. 25 Pinotepa de Don Luis, Oaxaca. 26 British Library, OIOC: Ad.Or.1714. 27 Photo Courtesy Whitworth Art Gallery, Manchester. 28 Collection Gösta Sandberg. 29 Ethnographic Museum, Göteborg. 30 National Museum of Denmark. 31 Swiss National Museum, Zurich. 32–35 CI. 36 Metropolitan Museum of Art, New York. 30.7.3 Anonymous gift, 1930. 37 National Museum of Denmark. 38 Courtesy: American Museum of Natural History, New York. 39, 40 MS. 41 Metropolitan Museum of Art, New York. 31.11.10. Fletcher Fund, 1931. 42 Jingzhou Prefecture Museum, Hubei Province. 43 Staatliche Antikensammlungen, Munich. 44 PMA. Purchased with the Bloomfield Moore Fund. 1933-50-1. 45 Acropolis Museum, Athens/Scala. 46 Hermitage Museum, St Petersburg. 47 Louvre, Paris. 48, 49 Hermitage Museum, St Petersburg. 50 National Museum, Naples. 51 © Xavier Renauld/Fondation EDF. 52 National Museum, Budapest. 53 Manchester Museum, University of Manchester. Photo Geoff Thompson. 54, 55 © University Museum of Cultural Heritage – University of Oslo, Norway. Photo Ove Holst. 56 Tomb 1 at Mashan, Jiangling, Hubei Province. 57 © Xavier Renauld/Fondation EDF. 58 PMA. Purchased with the Bloomfield Moore Fund 1934-5-6. 59 DB. 60 Priv. coll. 61, 62 DB. 63 Musée Historique des Tissus, Lyon. 64 Museum für Kunst und Gewerbe Hamburg. 65 St Ursula's Church, Cologne. 66 PMA. Purchased with John T. Morris Fund. 1951-90-1. 67 Cathedral Treasury, Uppsala. 68 Museo Sacro, Vatican. 69 Kunsthistorisches Museum, Vienna. 70 V&A, London. 1391-1904. 71, 72 Archivio de Obras Restauradas. I.P.H.E. Ministerio de Educación y Cultura. 73 PMA. Purchased from the Carl Shuster Collection with the John T. Morris Fund. 1940-4-647. 74 DB. 75 Shosoin Treasure House, Nara, Japan. 76 Museo Sacro, Vatican. 77 from L'Encyclopédie Diderot et D'Alambert: Arts Des Textiles, Plate VIII.

78 Museum of Fine Arts, Boston. 79 PMA. Gift of Howard L. Goodhart. 1936-14-1. 80 Louvre, Paris. 81 DB. 82 Photo Courtesy Simon Peers. 83 British Museum. MS 42130 f.202v. 84 Alte Kapelle, Regensburg. 85 PMA. Purchased with funds contributed by an anonymous donor. 1996-148-1a,b. 86, 87 CI. 88 Museum für Kunst und Gewerbe, Hamburg. 89 PMA. Purchased with the Joseph E. Temple Fund. 1939-21-5. 90 Courtesy Museo Diocesiano, Pienza/Scala. 91, 92 CI. 93 Musée de l'oeuvre Notre Dame de Strasbourg. 94 PMA. Purchased with Museum Funds. 1940-36-7. 95 Bibliothèque Forney, Paris. 96 PMA. Purchased with the Wandell Smith Fund. 1939-20-1. 97 Louvre, Paris. Inv. 2306, verso. 98 Bayerisches National Museum, Munich. 99 PMA. Purchased with funds contributed by Mr and Mrs Henry W. Breyer, Jr. 1967-71-4. 100 National Museum of Finland, Helsinki. 101 PMA, Bequest of Isabel Zucker. 1990-83-6. 102 PMA. Collection of Titus C. Geesey. 55-94-54. 103 PMA. Purchased with the Membership Fund. 1922-22-102. 104 PMA. Gift of Mrs George C. Thomas. 1922-29-2. 105 PMA. John D. McIlhenny Collection. 1943-40-67. 106 Royal Palace, Stockholm. 107 CI. 108 St Mary's Church, Gdansk. 109 MS. 110 Duke of Buccleugh, Boughton House. 111, 112 CI. 113 PMA. Bequest of Miss Elizabeth W. Lewis 1899-238. 114 PMA. John D. McIlhenny Collection. 1943-40-69. 115 Bowes Museum, Barnard Castle, County Durham, England. 116 PMA. Bequest of Miss Elizabeth W. Lewis. 1899-231. 117 ATA, Army Museum, Stockholm. 118 Leeds Museums and Art Galleries (Temple Newsam House)/Bridgeman Art Library. 119 CI. 120 PMA. Gift of the Friends of the PMA. 1988-7-4. 121 PMA. Gift of the children of Mrs Charles Custis Hamilton. 1929-175-3. 122 CI. 123 Warner Fabric Archives. 124 Jean-Paul Leclerc, Musées de la Mode et du Textile, Paris, coll. UCAD. 125 PMA. Purchased with Museum Funds 1876-62. 126 Textile Museum, Washington, D.C. 6.140. 127 PMA. Purchased from the Carl Shuster Collection with the John T. Morris Fund. 1940-4-850. 128 PMA. Purchased with the Offertory Fund. 1927-90-3. 129 Cliché Bibliothèque Nationale de France, Paris. 130 CI. 131 Department of Anthropology, National Museum of Natural History, Smithsonian Institution, Washington, D.C. Photo Larry Kirkland. 132 PMA. Gift of Hilda K. Watkins. 1985-79-1. 133 Priv. coll. 134 V&A, London. T.282-1987. Photo Daniel McGrath. 135 PMA. Gift of Mrs George W. Childs Drexel. 1939-1-19. 136 PMA. Purchased with the Art in Industry Fund. 1939-10-1. 137 PMA. The Henri Clouzot Collection, gift of Mrs Alfred Stengel. 1929-84-4. 138 PMA. Gift of Mr and Mrs Rodolphe Meyer de Schaunsee. 1951-68-28. 139 British Museum. MM42.11-12.13. 140 Auckland Museum. Photo Zrzysztof Pfeiffer. 141 Shosoin, Todaiji Temple, Nara, Japan. 142 Tokyo National Museum, Japan. 143 MS. 144 PMA. Purchased with the Costume and Textiles Revolving Fund. 1994-172-1. 145 PMA. Gift of Stella

Kramrisch 1961-102-2. 146 PMA. Gift of Mrs Hampton L. Carson. 1913-550. 147 Swiss National Museum, Zurich. AG-2369. 148 PMA. Gift of Miss G. B. Everett. 1912-99. 149 PMA. Gift of Mrs Edward Browning. 1950-3-4. 150 CI. 151 Nordiska Museum, Stockholm. 152 PMA. Gift of Mrs Morris Hawkes. 1945-13-4. 153 PMA. Gift of Mrs G. Craig Herberton. 1889-34. 154 PMA. Gift of Mrs Morris Hawkes. 1945-13-2. 155 Priv. coll. 156 PMA. Bequest of Mrs Harry Markoe. 1943-51-126. 157 PMA. Purchased with Museum Funds. 1992-82-38. 158 PMA. The Henri Clouzot Collection, gift of Mrs Alfred Stengel. 1929-144-11. 159 PMA. Purchased with the Mrs John T. Morris Fund. 1940-4-730. 160 PMA. Gifts of the Friends of the PMA. 1996-107-3. 161 PMA. Gift of Per Ebberston. 1923-40-1. 162 CI. 163 Hessische Hausstiftung, Kronberg. 164 Human History Department, Bolton Museum & Art Gallery. Photo John Parkinson Jones. 165 Pat Earnshaw. 166 PMA. Purchased with funds contributed by Mr and Mrs John Gilmore Ford. 1984-90-1. 167 Priv. coll. 168 Science Journal, December 1966. 169 PMA. The Samuel S. White 3rd and Vera White Collection. 1967-30-363. 170 Jean-Paul Leclerc, Musée de la Mode et du Textile, Paris, coll. UCAD. 171 Museum of London A.14395. 172 PMA. Gift of the Associate Committee of Women. 1894-30-72. 173 Musée Oberkampf, Jouy. 978.1.6a Gift of Mlle Biver. 174 Courtesy the Calico Printers Association, Ltd. 175 PMA. Gift of an anonymous donor. 1983-1a-d. 176 PMA. Gift of Mrs Thomas Raeburn White. 177 Photo Ron Barson. 178 from Diderot's Arts des Textiles: Travail au Ras au Métier, Plate II. 179 Centre de Documentació, Museu Textil, Terrassa. Inv. No. 12.521a/b. 180 Courtesy MS & Maclachlan Estate. 181 Macclesfield Silk Museums. 182 Penny Magazine, 1843. 183 Natural Museum of American History, Smithsonian Institution. 184 Strong Museum, Rochester, New York. 185 Hampshire County Council Museum Service. 186 Civiche Raccolte di Arte Applicata, Milan. 187 PMA. Gift of J. K. Nazare. 1928-44-1. 188 PMA. Gift of Mr and Mrs Richard Hautshorne Kimber. 1964-183-1. 189 Courtesy Grotta/Brown Gallery © Tom Grotta. 190 Warner Fabrics Archive. 191, 192 MS. 193 Courtesy of Central Saint Martins Museum & Study Collection. 194 Courtesy the Gift of the Friends of the PMA. 1988-7-6. 195 PMA. Gift of Furniture of the Twentieth Century, Inc. 1983-119-1. 196 MS. 197 Courtesy, Marlborough Gallery, New York. © Magdalena Abakanowicz. 198 Project realization and photos © Skyspan (Europe) GmbH. 199 Glasgow School of Art Collection. 200 Derby Museum & Art Gallery. 201 CI. 202 MS. 203 DB. 204 PMA. Gift of Nuno Corporation. 1995-95-1. 205 Courtesy John Picton. 206 Collection Victorian Tapestry Workshop. 207 Courtesy Tilleke Schwarz. 208 © Dean and Chapter of York: By kind permission. 209 Courtesy Judit-Kárpáti Rácz. 210 Courtesy Michael Brennand-Wood.

218

Acknowledgments

Writing this book has drawn on a lifetime's experience, much of it made possible by teachers, colleagues and friends. The first debt is to Jo Ann Stabb, who in her courses in fashion design and costume history at UCDavis, demonstrated why the smallest detail mattered and that designer-makers could also be good historians. Others who opened my mind – and doors to further opportunities – are Archie Brennan, George Donald, Robert Hildenbrand and Revel Oddy in Edinburgh, Connie Glenn and Pat Reeves in southern California, and, in London, Karen Finch, Valerie Mendez, Linda Parry and Kay Staniland. To St John Tibbitts I am especially indebted. He appointed me as the second Warner archivist and gave me my wings, establishing the mixture of archival work with writing, curating and lecturing that so enriched my nine years with the company and all the years since. He also facilitated the biography of – and thus friendship with – Marianne Straub, whose attitude to both life and cloth was truly inspiring. So too was Montse Stanley's, who allowed me entrée into the world of knitting. In their generosity, these and other company owners, collectors, curators and archivists too numerous to mention have enriched my firsthand acquaintance with historical textiles, while in studios, workshops and factories hundreds of practitioners have generously shared their expertise. To all of them I offer my deepest thanks.

While preparing this text, I have had helpful comments, advice and support from many people, among them Sylvia Backemeyer, David Bernstein, Sandy Black, Jane Bridgeman, Kirstie Buckland, Anna Buruma, Dilys Blum, Margot Coatts, Linda Eaton, Lynn Felsher, David Gazeley, Sem Longhurst, Diane MacKay, Lesley Miller, Maggie Millross, John Munro, John Picton, Fay Rance, Geraldine Rudge, Philip Sykas, Eleanor van Zandt and, especially, Sue Kerry and Annabel Westman, and John Gregory, who commented on the first draft. The sabbatical that made it possible was supported by a research fellowship from Central Saint Martins College of Art and Design, for which I am grateful to Jane Rapley, Dean of Fashion and Textiles. Finally, my thanks go gladly to the staff of Thames & Hudson, and to Terry McLean, whose love and laughter kept it all in perspective.